975.1
Ken

6517

DISCARDED

W9-BDD-941

DATE DUE

6517

Metro Litho
Oak Forest, IL 60452

975.1   Kent, Deborah
KEN   America the beautiful.
             Delaware

AMERICA the BEAUTIFUL

DELAWARE

By Deborah Kent

Consultants

Lewis E. Huffman, M.A., M.Ed; State Supervisor, Social Studies, Delaware Department of Public Instruction

Anne H. Cook, Editor, *Project 1776,* a Manual for the Bicentennial; Consultant to Brandywine Conservancy, Chadds Ford; former docent and guide, H. F. du Pont Winterthur Museum

Robert L. Hillerich, Ph.D., Bowling Green State University, Bowling Green, Ohio

CHILDRENS PRESS®
CHICAGO

HATHAWAY HIGH

Firemen go through their paces at the annual Fire Muster at Fort Christina Park, Wilmington.

Project Editor: Joan Downing
Associate Editor: Shari Joffe
Design Director: Margrit Fiddle
Typesetting: Graphic Connections, Inc.
Engraving: Liberty Photoengraving

Copyright © 1991 by Childrens Press®, Inc.
All rights reserved. Published simultaneously in Canada.
Printed in the United States of America.
1 2 3 4 5 6 7 8 9 10 R 00 99 98 97 96 95 94 93 92 91

Library of Congress Cataloging-in-Publication Data

Kent, Deborah.
    America the beautiful. Delaware / by Deborah Kent.
        p.   cm.
    Includes index.
    Summary: Introduces the geography, history, government, economy, industry, culture, historic sites, and famous people of Delaware.
    ISBN 0-516-00454-9
    1. Delaware—Juvenile literature.
[1. Delaware] I. Title.
F164.3.K46   1991   90-21116
975.1—dc20   CIP
                                                     AC

Old houses on
the Green, Dover

TABLE OF CONTENTS

Chapter 1

WELCOME
TO THE
FIRST STATE

WELCOME TO THE FIRST STATE

Crowds cheer and cameras flash as the inaugural procession moves grandly down Pennsylvania Avenue in Washington, D.C. A new president of the United States is about to take the oath of office. Behind the president and his entourage comes a parade of floats, limousines, and banners representing each state in the Union. Leading the way is the delegation from Delaware.

Delaware was the first state to ratify the United States Constitution in 1787. In honor of the unique role it played in the nation's history, Delaware has traditionally been granted first place when the fifty states are represented at national ceremonies.

For more than two centuries, Delaware has carried the nickname "First State." But the pride Delawareans feel goes beyond that long-ago moment when their state led the new nation to accept a lasting form of government. Although it is one of the smallest states in the Union, Delaware has launched some of the nation's most innovative programs of urban development. Its unemployment figures are among the lowest in the country. It has long been a leader in conducting scientific research.

Despite its size, Delaware is a state of surprising variety. Breakers crash across gleaming beaches, and bald eagles nest in a tangled cypress swamp. Delaware has thriving farms, lovely wooded hills, and humming factories. Traveling from the glass and steel office buildings of Wilmington to the old country manors of Sussex County, a visitor steps from one world into another.

Reflecting on Delaware's natural beauty, its prominence in industry, and its long and fascinating history, Delawareans call their state "a small wonder."

Chapter 2
THE LAND

THE LAND

*Delaware is like a diamond, diminutive,
but having within it inherent value.*
—John Lofland, "the Milford Bard," 1848

GEOGRAPHY AND TOPOGRAPHY

On a map, Delaware roughly resembles a shoe with its rounded toe kicking upward. The toe of the shoe is formed by Delaware's unique curved boundary with its northern neighbor, Pennsylvania. To the west and south, Delaware's straight borders with Maryland comprise the shoe's flat sole and squared-off heel. The eastern edge of Delaware is lapped by water—the Delaware River in the north, then Delaware Bay, and finally, from Cape Henlopen south to Fenwick Island, the Atlantic Ocean. New Jersey faces Delaware across the river and the bay. Covering 2,044 square miles (5,294 square kilometers), Delaware ranks forty-ninth in size among the fifty states. Only Rhode Island is smaller in area.

Delaware is located on the Delmarva Peninsula, a broad finger of land between the Atlantic Ocean and Chesapeake Bay. Delaware shares the peninsula with portions of Maryland and Virginia. The term Delmarva comes from the names of these three states. Delaware covers about one-third of the peninsula, which is also commonly referred to as Chesapeake Bay's Eastern Shore.

10

Dewey Beach is on the Atlantic Ocean between Cape Henlopen and Fenwick Island.

Nearly all of Delaware lies on the Atlantic Coastal Plain, a low, flat strip of land that extends from New Jersey to Florida. The land rises to rolling hills at the northern tip of the state, which is on the very edge of the Piedmont. The Piedmont is a wide plateau stretching along America's eastern seaboard from New Jersey to Alabama. Even on the Piedmont, Delaware's elevations are relatively low. The highest point in the state, near Centerville in northern New Castle County, measures only 442 feet (135 meters) above sea level.

LAKES AND RIVERS

Delaware has more than fifty freshwater lakes and ponds, most of them very small. The largest of these is Lums Pond, covering

Brandywine Creek near Montchanin

only 200 acres (81 hectares) near Kirkwood in New Castle County. Others include Killens Pond, south of Felton, and Trap Pond, in Sussex County east of Laurel.

The Delaware River, which flows along the state's northeastern edge, has played a major role in Delaware's economic development. Under the law, the bed and waters of the river up to the low-tide mark on the New Jersey side belong to Delaware. This fact created some complex legal problems during the 1980s. For more than fifty years, sediment from dredging the river channel had been heaped on the New Jersey side, until it finally spilled over the low-tide line into Delaware's territory. Both states claimed these landfill areas, but a court ruling decided in Delaware's favor.

The Christina, the largest river entirely within the state, meets Brandywine Creek at Wilmington and flows eastward to join the Delaware. Its mouth forms Wilmington Harbor. The

Waterfowl at Bombay Hook National Wildlife Refuge

Appoquinimink and the Smyrna are also tributaries of the
Delaware River. The St. Jones, Mispillion, and Broadkill rivers
empty into Delaware Bay. Rising in southwestern Delaware, the
Nanticoke and the Choptank flow west across Maryland to reach
Chesapeake Bay.

COAST AND WETLANDS

Delaware has about 28 miles (45 kilometers) of Atlantic
coastline, extending from Fenwick Island, on the Maryland
border, to Cape Henlopen, at the mouth of Delaware Bay. A long
sandbar, or sand reef, off the mainland forms Delaware's most
popular beaches, including Bethany Beach, Dewey Beach, and
Rehoboth Beach. Behind the sand reef lie Rehoboth Bay, Indian
River Bay, and Little Assawoman Bay.

To the north, the shore of Delaware Bay is a patchwork of

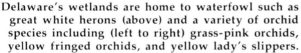
Delaware's wetlands are home to waterfowl such as great white herons (above) and a variety of orchid species including (left to right) grass-pink orchids, yellow fringed orchids, and yellow lady's slippers.

beaches and salt marshes. At Prime Hook and Bombay Hook National Wildlife Refuges, some of the wetlands along the bay are protected from development.

Away from the ocean, at the southern edge of Sussex County, the last remnants of the Great Pocomoke Swamp struggle for survival. During the eighteenth century, the swamp sprawled over more than 50,000 acres (20,234 hectares) of land in Delaware and Maryland, but much of it has been drained to produce fertile farmland. In Sussex County, about 11,000 acres (4,452 hectares) of swampland called Great Cypress Swamp now belong to Delaware Wild Lands, a private conservation organization that is dedicated to preserving this unique ecosystem.

PLANT AND ANIMAL LIFE

Many trees are native to Delaware, including hickories, yellow poplars, beeches, sycamores, shortleaf pines, and several varieties of oak. Some farmers earn extra money in the winter by gathering branches of the American holly, Delaware's state tree, and weaving them into Christmas wreaths. Red cedars flourish in the Great Pocomoke Swamp, which is also the northernmost limit in the range of the bald cypress. Several rare orchid species can be found in the state's wetlands, as well as jack-in-the-pulpits, skunk cabbages, and water lilies. In the woodlands, a hiker may spot lady's slippers, bloodroots, hepaticas, and violets.

Commercial fishermen harvest Delaware Bay's valuable crabs, clams, lobsters, sea bass, and sea trout.

Delaware's woods and wetlands are home to white-tailed deer and to such smaller mammals as red foxes, gray foxes, raccoons, skunks, and opossums. Muskrats, otters, and minks inhabit the wetlands. A few pairs of bald eagles nest in the Pocomoke Swamp, as do several rare species of warblers. Vast colonies of herons, egrets, and ibises thrive in the wetlands along Delaware Bay.

Whales are occasionally sighted off the Atlantic Coast, and schools of porpoises sometimes cavort in Delaware Bay. The crabs, clams, and oysters that are harvested along the shore are a mainstay in Delaware's cuisine.

New Castle County receives more snowfall than any other part of the state.

CLIMATE

Fanned in the summer by ocean breezes and warmed in winter by the Gulf Stream, Delaware's Atlantic Coast enjoys a gentle climate. Farther inland, however, summers tend to be hot and humid, and winters furnish plenty of sleet and snow. New Castle County, in the north, receives more snowfall than any other part of the state—about 18 inches (46 centimeters) per year, compared with only 12 inches (30 centimeters) on the coast. Overall, Delaware gets about 46 inches (117 centimeters) of precipitation— a combination of rain and melted snow—each year.

January temperatures in Delaware average 35 degrees Fahrenheit (2 degrees Celsius). The average temperature in July is a balmy 76 degrees Fahrenheit (24 degrees Celsius). The town of Millsboro holds the record for both the state's all-time high and all-time low temperature readings—110 degrees Fahrenheit (43 degrees Celsius) on July 21, 1930, and minus 17 degrees Fahrenheit (minus 27 degrees Celsius) on January 17, 1893.

17

Chapter 3
THE PEOPLE

THE PEOPLE

A century ago, an Episcopalian bishop in Delaware remarked that "the ideal Delawarean is born in Sussex County, has Rodney and Burton grandfathers so that he is related to everybody, marries a Ridgely of Dover for his first wife and a Corbit of Odessa for his second, [and] lives . . . in Wilmington." A handful of families have remained prominent throughout Delaware's history, and, in such a small state, people often get the feeling that they know everyone else. Yet Delawareans come from many backgrounds, and the state today has far more ethnic variety than the bishop could have imagined.

POPULATION

With 594,338 people according to the 1980 census, Delaware ranks forty-seventh in population among the fifty states. Only Alaska, Vermont, and Wyoming have fewer people. The population of the entire state of Delaware is only about one-third that of the city of Philadelphia. About 71 percent of all Delawareans are classified as urban dwellers, living in towns of at least 2,500 people. The remaining 29 percent live on farms or in small towns.

Wilmington is the only big city in Delaware. About two-thirds of the people in the state live in Wilmington or its metropolitan area. Newark, home of the University of Delaware, is the state's second-largest city. Dover, the state capital, ranks third in population.

This Newark schoolyard is located in New Castle County, the most densely populated part of the state.

New Castle County, which forms Delaware's northern tip, is the most heavily industrialized and densely populated part of the state. The southern counties of Kent and Sussex are largely devoted to farmland, with a scattering of small towns. This difference between northern and southern Delaware has molded the history and culture of the state.

WHO ARE THE DELAWAREANS?

The first Europeans to settle Delaware were people from Sweden, The Netherlands, and England. Many old Swedish, Dutch, and English family names can still be heard throughout the state. About 97 percent of today's Delawareans were born in the United States. Among Delaware's foreign-born residents are people from Great Britain, Canada, Italy, and Poland. Small

These young people dressed in Swedish costumes were photographed at Old Swedes Church during the 350th anniversary celebration of the Swedish settlers' landing in Delaware.

numbers of Hispanics (most of them from Puerto Rico) and Asians have settled in the Wilmington area. A few descendants of the Nanticoke Indians, one of Delaware's original Native American groups, still live in the southwestern corner of the state.

Black people comprise about 14 percent of Delaware's population. Most black Delawareans live in or near Wilmington, but some live in rural areas, where they work as farmers or fishermen.

RELIGION AND POLITICS

The town of Frederica is sometimes called the "Cradle of Methodism in America." At a historic meeting here in 1784, two English Methodist leaders organized America's Methodist Episcopal church. In the decades that followed, Delaware served

22

The young girls riding their bicycles (above) and the Nanticoke Indians shown here at their annual powwow (left) are among the 97 percent of Delawareans who were born in the United States.

as a springboard for the spread of Methodism throughout the United States.

Roman Catholics comprise the largest single religious denomination in the state. Other churches in the state include Lutheran, Baptist, Episcopalian, and Presbyterian. The Jewish population is centered in Wilmington and a few of its suburbs.

In politics, Delawareans have tended to vote Republican throughout most of the twentieth century. Republican presidential candidates have won Delaware's electoral votes twice as often as have Democrats. Between 1960 and 1990, however, Delawareans elected three Democratic governors, compared with only two chosen over the previous sixty years. In general, the people of Wilmington tend to vote for Democratic candidates, as do rural blacks and whites. The Republican party is strongest in the affluent suburbs of New Castle County.

Chapter 4
THE BEGINNING

THE BEGINNING

He hath found the said country full of trees, to wit, oaks,
hickories, and pines. . . . He hath seen, in the said
country, bucks and does, turkeys and partridges. He hath
found the climate of said country very temperate, judging it
to be as temperate as the climate of this country Holland.
—From the report of Dutch explorer Cornelius Hendricksen, 1616.

THE FIRST DELAWAREANS

When Europeans reached Delaware early in the 1600s, they
found the scattered villages of a group of Indians who called
themselves the Lenape, meaning the "ordinary people." The
Lenape lived in today's states of Delaware and New Jersey and in
parts of eastern Pennsylvania. Their dome-shaped houses were
built of bent saplings and plastered with mud and cornhusks.
They traveled the streams and rivers in dugout canoes. Lenape
women tended gardens in which they raised corn, beans, and
squash, while the men fished and hunted.

The Lenape belonged to the large Algonquian family of eastern
tribes, related to one another by similar languages and customs.
Like the people of many other Algonquian groups, the Lenape
traced their descent through their mother's families. Women
played an important role in tribal government.

Several other Native American groups lived in parts of present-
day Sussex County. The strongest of these were the Nanticokes,

English navigator Henry Hudson, the first European to reach Delaware, sailed the *Half Moon* (above) into Delaware Bay in 1609.

who were heavily concentrated along Chesapeake Bay to the west. The Lenape and the Nanticokes were both dominated by the powerful Susquehannocks, who lived in what is now Pennsylvania and sometimes sent raiding parties into the south.

THE COMING OF THE DUTCH

Most historians agree that the first European to reach Delaware was English navigator Henry Hudson. Hudson had been hired by the Dutch to search for a "Northwest Passage," a waterway across North America to Asia. In 1609, Hudson's ship, the *Half Moon*, sailed into Delaware Bay. Hudson and his crew explored the bay and discovered the mouth of the Delaware River. Realizing that Delaware Bay was not the Northwest Passage he sought, Hudson headed north along the Atlantic Coast until he found the river that now bears his name.

The following year, a sea captain named Samuel Argall, from the English colony of Virginia, was swept off course by a violent storm and took refuge in the bay Hudson had discovered. Argall named the bay De La Warr after Lord De La Warr, governor of Virginia. Eventually, the name, later spelled Delaware, was also given to the large river that flowed into the bay, to the land along the bay's western shore, and to the Lenape Indians.

Inspired by Hudson's discoveries, the Dutch sent several more expeditions to explore the land around Delaware Bay. Cornelius Mey in 1614 and Cornelius Hendricksen in 1616 reported that the land teemed with beavers and other animals. They claimed that the Indians were eager to trade furs for kettles, muskets, and rum. The merchants of the Dutch West India Company were intrigued, and determined to harvest Delaware's riches.

In 1631, a band of about three dozen Dutch settlers disembarked from the ship *Walvis* (meaning whale) near the present-day town of Lewes at the mouth of Delaware Bay. Sponsored by the Dutch West India Company, they intended to farm, send out whaling expeditions, and trade with the Indians for furs. The settlers built a fort surrounded by a sturdy log palisade and christened their tiny colony Zwaanendael, which means Valley of the Swans. One of the sponsors later wrote that "their cows calved and their fields were seeded and covered with a fine crop."

Zwaanendael might have flourished, and the Dutch might have secured a firm toehold in Delaware, if it had not been for one of those odd accidents of history. The trouble arose because someone mounted a tin shield bearing a coat of arms on a stake outside the fort. The neighboring Indians were fascinated by all forms of metal, which they had rarely seen before. Soon a young brave carried the coat of arms back to his village. The colonists were outraged. They made such a fuss that the Lenape chief (who

In the spring of 1631, about three dozen Dutch settlers sponsored by the Dutch West India Company landed at Zwaanendael, near Lewes (above).

desperately wanted the Dutch as allies against the Susquehannocks) finally had the thief put to death. To avenge him, the dead brave's friends attacked Zwaanendael and murdered the settlers. Only one man survived to tell the story.

New Sweden settlers traded with the Delaware Indians.

The Zwaanendael raid was the only serious battle fought in Delaware between Indians and Europeans. Pressured by the Susquehannocks and weakened by smallpox and other European diseases, for which they had no natural immunity, the Lenape left Delaware by about 1690.

NEW SWEDEN

Six years after the massacre at Zwaanendael, two shiploads of colonists sailed up the Delaware River. Where a broad stream emptied into the Delaware, the ships found a fine harbor. About half of the colonists came from Sweden, and they named this tributary of the Delaware for their monarch, Queen Christina. According to legend, the colonists clambered ashore on a stony ledge known to this day as The Rocks.

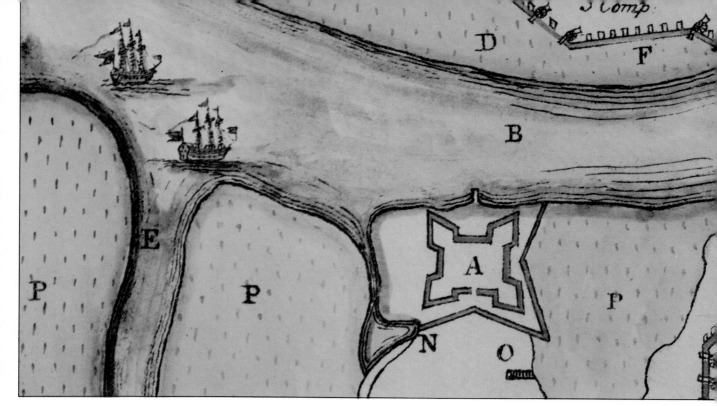

Fort Christina (A) became the first permanent white settlement in Delaware.

Directed by their leader, Peter Minuit, the colonists built Fort Christina at the site of present-day Wilmington. Fort Christina became the first permanent white settlement on Delaware soil.

The colony at Fort Christina began as a joint venture between The Netherlands and Sweden. But the Dutch soon withdrew, devoting their energy to the New Amsterdam colony on the Hudson. Fort Christina emerged as the heart of New Sweden, a string of settlements along the Delaware River from present-day Wilmington nearly to Philadelphia.

From the outset, New Sweden's future was clouded. The Dutch resented the colony as a threat to New Amsterdam, and the British were hungry to claim the entire Atlantic Coast as their territory. Yet under the able leadership of Governor Johan Printz, New Sweden managed to expand. An enormous man who weighed nearly 400 pounds (181 kilograms), Printz encouraged industry in

This replica of one of the original Swedish log cabins is located in Fort Christina Park, near Wilmington.

the colony. Soon millers, weavers, bakers, and brewers were hard at work. Lured by the promise of muskets and other goods, Indians brought valuable beaver pelts to the Swedish trading posts. The Swedish colonists built sturdy cabins of logs that kept out the winter gales far better than the lumber houses used in the British colonies. These Swedish homes were the first log cabins of the American frontier.

In 1651, alarmed by Sweden's growing strength at their doorstep, the Dutch built Fort Casimir at the site of present-day New Castle. Under Johan Rising, the Swedes captured the fort three years later. But their victory was shortlived. In 1655, New Netherland's governor, Peter Stuyvesant, recaptured Fort Casimir and took Fort Christina as well. The Swedish colonists were allowed to keep their property and to practice their Lutheran faith, but the days of New Sweden were over.

In 1664, the English took possession of the Dutch colonies in the New World. Peter Stuyvesant (with cane) was forced to surrender New Amsterdam.

THE THREE LOWER COUNTIES

Over the next few years, a Dutch settlement named New Amstel grew up around Fort Casimir. The soldiers sent to man the fort spent more time tending gardens than marching on maneuvers, and the fort fell into disrepair.

For decades, England had coveted the Dutch colonies in the New World. In 1664, the British king, Charles II, granted all of the territory east of the Delaware River to his brother James, Duke of York. British warships captured New Amsterdam after barely a struggle, and forces under the command of Sir Robert Carr swept the drowsy settlement at New Amstel. The British rechristened New Amstel, naming it New Castle.

In 1681, Charles II made another gift of land in the New World, this time to William Penn, the son of one of his father's loyal

Quaker William Penn landed in Pennsylvania in 1682.

supporters. Penn's land grant covered today's state of
Pennsylvania. Not wanting to infringe on the Duke of York's
territory, the king ordered that a curved boundary be drawn
within a 12-mile (19-kilometer) radius of the spire of New Castle
Court House.

William Penn was a devout member of the Society of Friends, or
Quakers, a religious group that had been persecuted in England
for its beliefs. Quakers were pacifists, opposing all warfare and
military service. Penn dreamed of founding an American colony
according to his Quaker principles.

From Penn's point of view, the king's grant had only one
drawback—it offered no direct access to the Atlantic Ocean. Penn
appealed to the Duke of York, the king's brother. The duke gave
Penn all of his land that lay west of the Delaware River from Cape
Henlopen to the circular line above New Castle. The deed granted
the land to Penn and his descendants for ten thousand years.

Between 1685 and 1699, pirates prowled Delaware Bay and plundered villages near the shores.

At first, Penn tried to govern Pennsylvania and its "three lower counties" of New Castle, Kent, and Sussex as a single territory. Almost from the start, however, people in the Lower Counties were discontent. They resented the nonviolent Pennsylvania Quakers, who offered no resistance when pirates began to prowl Delaware Bay, attacking merchant ships and plundering villages. They also felt overwhelmed by Philadelphia, which grew ever larger and more important as a commercial center. In the Lower Counties, people complained that their voices could not be heard in the General Assembly. Finally, in 1701, Penn agreed to let the Lower Counties have their own assembly at New Castle.

Technically, the Lower Counties remained part of Pennsylvania. But over the years they acted more and more on their own. In 1757, a New Castle assemblyman wrote, "We are independent of [Pennsylvania], which we esteem no small part of our happiness, and we will ever assert and support that independency."

Many Delaware farmers and landowners prospered during the 1700s.

The farms and forests of the Lower Counties produced an
abundance of beef, cheese, grain, and lumber for export to
Philadelphia and to the West Indies. Wealthy landholders
throughout the province, especially those in the south, depended
on African slaves to work their farms. Many people in the colony
fiercely opposed slavery. Yet the institution had existed in
Delaware since the time of Governor Printz and was thoroughly
entrenched by the mid-1700s.

In 1731, a Quaker merchant from Philadelphia named Thomas
Willing settled near old Fort Christina. There he went into
business, exchanging farm produce for a variety of imported
goods. More Quakers joined him, as did a number of Scotch-Irish
immigrants. The Scotch-Irish were Scottish families who had lived
for several generations in Ireland. At first, the growing
community was called Willingtown, but in 1739 the name was

The Fenwick Island
Mason and Dixon Line
marker still stands.

changed to Wilmington. By 1775, with twelve hundred
inhabitants, Wilmington was the biggest town in the province.

For decades, Delaware and the neighboring Maryland colony
had quarreled over the land south of Cape Henlopen. In 1765, two
English surveyors, Charles Mason and Jeremiah Dixon, marked
Delaware's southern and western boundaries, putting an end to
the dispute. Mason and Dixon's Line greatly increased Delaware's
territory by adding a large tract of land to Sussex County.
A century later, this line would divide a troubled nation.

THE WAR FOR INDEPENDENCE

The thirteen British colonies had grown used to conducting
their business with little interference from the mother country.
But during the 1700s, England was embroiled in a series of costly

Colonists burn stamps to protest the Stamp Act, a measure passed by the British Parliament as a means of taxing the American colonies.

wars with France. In 1765, members of Parliament voted to raise money by taxing the colonies in the New World. They began by passing the Stamp Act, which required colonists to buy an official stamp for all legal documents, newspapers, and even playing cards.

In October 1765, two Delaware delegates—Caesar Rodney of Jones's Neck, and Thomas McKean of New Castle—attended a congress in New York to protest the Stamp Act. Parliament quickly repealed the Stamp Act but replaced it with the Townshend Acts, a series of taxes on such imported items as lead, paint, paper, and tea. When Philadelphia merchants organized a boycott of British goods, they won Delaware's firm support.

Tension continued to mount between Great Britain and the colonies. In 1774, Caesar Rodney, Thomas McKean, and George Read represented Delaware at the First Continental Congress in

George Read (left), Caesar Rodney (above), and Thomas McKean, who were Continental Congress representatives from Delaware, all signed the Declaration of Independence.

Philadelphia, which petitioned Parliament and the king for relief from the tax burden. Then, in April 1775, news reached Delaware that British troops had fired on a band of colonial militia at Lexington, Massachusetts. The colonies began to arm for war.

Within months, Delaware organized a Council of Safety to oversee defense. Under Colonel John Haslet, the Council of Safety recruited Delaware's first regiment for the Continental army.

In the spring of 1776, McKean, Read, and Rodney attended the Second Continental Congress. For years, most people in the colonies had hoped to keep their ties to Great Britain, reconciling their differences peacefully. But on July 1, the congress opened discussion on a bold resolution that would make the colonies independent.

After hours of heated debate, the congress voted on the independence resolution. Thomas McKean voted for

This statue of Caesar Rodney in Wilmington commemorates Rodney's historic 1776 ride.

independence. George Read, influenced by his friend John Dickinson (a former Delawarean who now represented Pennsylvania), was opposed, still arguing for reconciliation.

Caesar Rodney was not present when this first vote was taken. He had returned to Delaware to deal with an armed uprising of British loyalists. But on the bleak, stormy night of July 1, he set out from Dover on horseback for Philadelphia. Although he was in poor health due to asthma and skin cancer, Rodney galloped all night, pausing only to change horses. After 80 bone-jarring miles (129 kilometers), he reached Philadelphia in time to cast his vote for independence.

With two delegates for independence and only one still against, Delaware joined the rest of the colonies in a united decision to

40

Delaware troops leaving the Dover Green in 1776 to fight in the Revolutionary War

break the bond with England. On July 4, the Delaware delegation signed the Declaration of Independence.

Not only did Delaware separate from Great Britain in 1776, it also cut its final ties with Pennsylvania. In August, George Read presided over a constitutional convention in New Castle, the first such convention held in any American state. The first constitution of the "Delaware State" called for an elected chief executive, or president, and a two-chamber legislature. It also banned the importation of slaves and guaranteed freedom of religion and freedom of the press.

The valor of Delaware's troops during the Revolutionary War earned them an unusual nickname—the "Blue Hen's Chickens." When time hung heavy on their hands, the soldiers often

41

entertained themselves with cockfights. According to legend, one man brought along some gamecocks that were the descendants of a blue hen famous in Kent County. Few other birds could outfight the blue hen's chickens. The name soon stuck to Haslet's Delaware regiment.

Little actual fighting took place on Delaware soil. In September 1777, colonial troops under William Maxwell held off the British for three days at Cooch's Bridge near Newark. But after heavy casualties, Maxwell was forced to retreat. A week later, the British seized Wilmington and captured Delaware's president, John McKinly. Soon afterward, the British fleet anchored off New Castle on its way up the Delaware River to Philadelphia. In December 1777, the state assembly moved out of harm's way to Dover, in Kent County. Dover has been Delaware's capital ever since.

THE FIRST STATE

In 1783, British and American representatives signed a peace treaty that ended the Revolutionary War and granted American independence. Now the new nation faced the challenge of devising a just and practical means of governing itself.

During the summer of 1787, delegates from each of the thirteen states held a Constitutional Convention in Philadelphia. The Delaware delegation consisted of George Read, Richard Bassett, Gunning Bedford, Jr., Jacob Broom, and John Dickinson (recently returned from Pennsylvania). Delawareans feared their small state would be overwhelmed by larger states such as New York, Pennsylvania, and Virginia. The Delaware delegates fiercely opposed the "Virginia Plan," which based representation in Congress strictly on population. Led by John Dickinson, Delaware

On December 7, 1787, Delaware delegates ratified the United States Constitution in the Council Room of Battell's Tavern, Dover.

supported the "Great Compromise," a plan promoted by several of the smaller states. Under the compromise, each state — regardless of size — would send two senators to the upper house of Congress. Representation in the lower house would be determined by population.

When the Great Compromise was accepted by the Constitutional Convention, the Delaware delegates rushed back to Dover with the news. A state convention met to decide whether Delaware should accept the Constitution's terms. On December 7, 1787, after only four days of discussion, Delaware became the first state to approve, or ratify, the United States Constitution.

Chapter 5
GROWING AND CHANGING

GROWING AND CHANGING

*After having seen, nearly half a century ago,
the banks of the Brandywine a scene of bloody
fighting, I am happy now to find upon them the seat
of industry, beauty, and mutual friendship.*
— the Marquis de Lafayette, writing in a young girl's
album during his visit to the United States, 1824

THE RISE OF INDUSTRY

On January 1, 1800, the first day of a new century, a French
writer named Pierre Samuel du Pont de Nemours arrived in the
United States with his son Éleuthère Irénée. Du Pont was
disillusioned with the revolution in France, which had promised
equality and brotherhood but led only to bloodshed. He hoped
that the United States would offer his family opportunities
unimagined in his homeland.

Éleuthère Irénée du Pont was a young man of energy and ideas.
He had worked at a powder mill in France and quickly realized
that American gunpowder was overpriced and of poor quality. In
1802, he began to manufacture gunpowder at Eleutherian Mills on
Brandywine Creek not far from Wilmington.

Demand for du Pont's powder soared when war broke out
between the United States and Great Britain in 1812. American
military authorities feared that the Eleutherian Mills would be a
prime target for British attack.

46

Eleutherian Mills on Brandywine Creek stands on the original site where E. I. du Pont began his powder mill in 1802.

The enemy never reached Brandywine Creek, but in April 1813, a British squadron attacked the port of Lewes at the mouth of Delaware Bay. For twenty-two hours, British vessels hurled cannonballs at the town. Lewes was well defended, however, and the British could not get close enough to do any real damage. Afterward, a popular rhyme gloated, ''The British commander and all his men / Shot a dog and killed a hen.''

Farming remained the backbone of Delaware's economy in the nineteenth century. Little by little, however, manufacturing grew in importance. In addition to providing waterpower for the manufacture of powder, Brandywine Creek turned sawmills and flour mills. Brandywine flour was famous for its softness and whiteness. Paper mills operated on Brandywine and White Clay creeks. Wilmington gained a reputation for making leather goods

The Chesapeake and Delaware Canal, a waterway between Chesapeake Bay and the Delaware River, spared cargo ships a long voyage around the Delmarva Peninsula.

and fine carriages. To the south, at Millsboro, smoke rose from roaring iron furnaces.

Lying midway between Philadelphia and the new federal capital at Washington, Delaware occupied a strategic position. As early as 1790, John Fitch operated steamboats between Wilmington and Philadelphia. By 1812, several steamboat companies carried passengers up and down the Delaware River. In 1824, workers began a five-year construction project, digging and blasting their way across the Eastern Shore to create the Chesapeake and Delaware (C & D) Canal. A waterway from Chesapeake Bay to the Delaware River, the canal spared cargo ships a 285-mile (459-kilometer) voyage around the Delmarva Peninsula. Spanning the state south of New Castle, the C & D Canal has traditionally been regarded as the division between northern and southern Delaware.

A bird's-eye view of Wilmington about the time of the Civil War

STORM CLOUDS ON THE HORIZON

"Slavery in a republic or free government is a paradox," proclaimed a letter to the editor of a Wilmington newspaper in 1795. Many Delawareans, especially the state's Quakers and Methodists, echoed these sentiments. In speeches throughout the nation during the 1790s, Warner Mifflin of Mifflin's Cross Roads (present-day Camden) urged that slavery be abolished.

By 1790, black people made up about 20 percent of Delaware's total population. About one-third of the blacks in the state were free. Over the decades that followed, more and more slaveholders, including such Delaware leaders as Richard Bassett and John Dickinson, freed their slaves. Some free blacks went into business as barbers, millers, or fishermen, while others worked as farm laborers. In Delaware, free blacks were allowed to testify in trials, a right they lacked in most other slave states. Delaware was the only slave state in which the courts automatically considered a black person to be free unless she or he could be proved a slave.

The conditions for free blacks and slaves were less harsh in Delaware than they were in the states farther south. Yet even here, black people endured daily restrictions and humiliations. Blacks were forbidden to marry whites or to carry firearms. Free blacks were not permitted to move into Delaware, even if members of their families lived in the state.

Worse still, some unscrupulous slave dealers captured free blacks and sold them in southern states. Lucretia "Patty" Cannon headed a gang of ruffians who seized unsuspecting men, women, and children as they worked in the fields or walked on lonely country roads. Over a period of forty years, she and her band kidnapped hundreds of people, chaining them in the attic of the tavern she operated in Reliance on the Maryland line. Patty Cannon was finally arrested in 1829 and died in a Georgetown jail.

While Patty Cannon smuggled free black people into the South, "station masters" on the Underground Railroad helped runaway slaves to reach freedom in the northern states. The Underground Railroad was a secret system of "stations," or safe houses, where escaping slaves could hide during their perilous journey. During his years with the Underground Railroad, Thomas Garrett, a Quaker iron merchant from Wilmington, assisted about three thousand runaways. In 1848, two Maryland slaveholders sued Garrett for damages, and he stood trial in New Castle. Garrett was convicted and sentenced to pay a heavy fine. "Judge," he declared, "thou hast not left me a dollar, but I . . . say to thee, and to all in this courtroom, that if anyone knows of a fugitive who wants shelter . . . send him to Thomas Garrett and he will befriend him."

LIBERTY LINE.

NEW ARRANGEMENT---NIGHT AND DAY.

The improved and splendid Locomotives, Clarkson and Lundy, with their trains fitted up in the best style of accommodation for passengers, will run their regular trips during the present season, between the borders of the Patriarchal Dominion and Libertyville, Upper Canada. Gentlemen and Ladies, who may wish to improve their health or circumstances, by a northern tour, are respectfully invited to give us their patronage.

SEATS FREE, *irrespective of color.*

Necessary Clothing furnished gratuitously to such as have *"fallen among thieves."*

"Hide the outcasts—let the oppressed go free."—*Bible.*

For seats apply at any of the trap doors, or to the conductor of the train.

J. CROSS, *Proprietor.*

N. B. For the special benefit of Pro-Slavery Police Officers, an extra heavy wagon for Texas, will be furnished, whenever it may be necessary, in which they will be forwarded as dead freight, to the "Valley of Rascals," always at the risk of the owners.

Extra Overcoats provided for such of them as are afflicted with protracted *chilly-phobia.*

This advertisement for the Underground Railroad appeared in the July 13, 1844 edition of the *Western Citizen.*

INTO CIVIL WAR

As tension over the slavery issue mounted throughout the nation, Delaware was painfully divided. Although slavery had declined steadily in the state, many people in Sussex and Kent counties sympathized with the South. Antislavery feeling was strong, however, in industrial New Castle County.

In 1860, Abraham Lincoln ran for president with the antislavery Republican party. Delaware gave its electoral votes to Vice-President John Cabell Breckinridge, a southern Democrat. To the consternation of the southern states, Lincoln won the election. Within months, eleven southern states seceded from the Union to form their own nation, the Confederate States of America.

During the Civil War, Fort Delaware held about 12,500 Confederate prisoners of war.

Delaware's governor, William Burton, was a Democrat with strong southern leanings. Fired by Confederate speeches, he pressed the legislature to call for a convention that would consider secession. The legislature refused. At a rally in 1861, John W. Houston, a former congressman, exhorted his audience to "stay at home in the Union until the crack of doom, or until it goes to pieces . . . and we are left standing solitary and alone with our feet planted firmly on the rock of the Constitution . . . as the last survivors of the federation of the American states!"

Delaware did stay in the Union, but its citizens remained divided in their loyalties. Hundreds of Delaware men went south to put on the gray uniforms of Confederate soldiers. Some Delawareans smuggled food and other supplies to the southern troops. To prevent further problems, Lincoln suspended the constitutional rights of Delawareans during the war. He ordered

The interior of Fort Delaware, on Pea Patch Island

federal troops to monitor elections within the state and disarmed prosouthern militia companies. Dozens of Delawareans were arrested and held prisoner without trial, simply on suspicion of treason. On one occasion, twenty-five New Castle men and women were jailed simply for organizing a picnic to raise money to buy food for the prisoners at Fort Delaware.

At one time, the infamous Fort Delaware, on tiny Pea Patch Island, held many suspect Delaware citizens, as well as 12,500 Confederate prisoners of war. Some prisoners were kept in cold, damp, underground cells. Hunger and disease were rampant. By war's end, about 2,400 prisoners had perished.

Though some Delawareans continued to support the southern cause, thousands of Delaware volunteers served the Union during the long years of the war. Nearly one-third of the men in General Henry Lockwood's Delaware unit died at the bloody Battle of

Delaware naval officer Samuel Francis du Pont (second from left) helped to plan Union strategies during the Civil War.

Antietam. Thomas A. Smyth, an Irish Catholic from Wilmington, rose through the ranks to become a brigadier general. He was killed on April 7, 1865, only days before the final truce. Distinguished naval officer Samuel F. du Pont helped to plan crucial Union strategies.

Delaware industries also aided in the war effort. The du Pont mills on Brandywine Creek produced more than a third of the gunpowder used by the Union army. Wilmington shipyards assembled naval vessels, and carriage makers began turning out heavy military wagons.

On January 1, 1863, Lincoln delivered the Emancipation Proclamation, granting freedom to all slaves in Confederate territory. Slaves in the Union states, however, were not affected. Delaware and Kentucky were the last states to free their slaves,

The du Pont powder mills on Brandywine Creek produced more than a third of the gunpowder used by the Union army.

when the Thirteenth Amendment to the Constitution made slavery illegal in 1865.

POLITICS AND COMMERCE

In 1874, the Reverend Isaac William Handy published a book recounting the horrors he had experienced as a prisoner at Fort Delaware. Due to a false rumor that he had served as a chaplain for the Confederacy, he had been arrested and imprisoned without a trial, and held for fifteen months. Handy's story, and the memories of hundreds of other Delawareans whose constitutional rights had been violated during the war, kept anti-Union feeling strong in Delaware for decades. In Congress, Delaware voted with the "Solid South," and at home the state legislature adopted a policy based on the notion of white supremacy. "The immutable laws of God have affixed upon the brows of the white races the ineffaceable stamp of superiority," declared one state legislator in the 1870s. "All attempt to elevate the Negro to social or political equality . . . is futile and subversive."

Many white Delawareans, however, believed that black people must have greater opportunities. In 1866, a Wilmington Quaker named Thomas Kimber headed a group of doctors, lawyers, and clergymen to form the Delaware Association for the Moral Improvement and Education of the Colored People. This association, as well as the federal government's Freedmen's Bureau, set up schools for black children and helped former slaves to find jobs. Black tradesmen and church groups also raised funds for schools and training programs.

During the 1870s and 1880s, Delaware was essentially a one-party state. The Democratic party, led by a few wealthy families such as the Bayards and the Saulsburys, controlled the General Assembly. Since blacks generally supported the Republicans, the Democrats manipulated state laws to prevent most blacks from voting. Republicans grew so discouraged that in the election years of 1878 and 1886 they did not even nominate a slate of candidates.

The two-party system revived in Delaware with a boost from John Edward Addicks, a Republican millionaire from Claymont. Because he had made his fortune by owning and manipulating gas companies, he was nicknamed "Gas Addicks." In 1888, Addicks began to pour money into Republican campaigns. With his help, Joshua Marvil was elected governor, the first Republican to hold that office since the Civil War. However, despite all his efforts, Addicks never fulfilled his personal ambition of becoming one of Delaware's United States senators.

One of the many Wilmington industries that thrived in the 1800s was the Bancroft Mills, founded in 1831 by Joseph Bancroft to spin and weave cotton.

During the last decades of the nineteenth century, improved transportation by rail and steamship enabled Delaware farmers to export their produce up and down the Atlantic Coast. Farmers raised a variety of crops for sale, including peaches, strawberries, and melons.

The late 1800s also heralded increasing diversity in Delaware industries. Wilmington grew in importance as a factory center, producing paper, vulcanized fiber for electrical insulation, and goatskin leather, called kid, for shoes. The Du Pont Company remained at the forefront of explosives manufacturing. By the dawn of the twentieth century, the du Pont family had amassed a fortune, and had become a powerful and positive force in Delaware's social and political development.

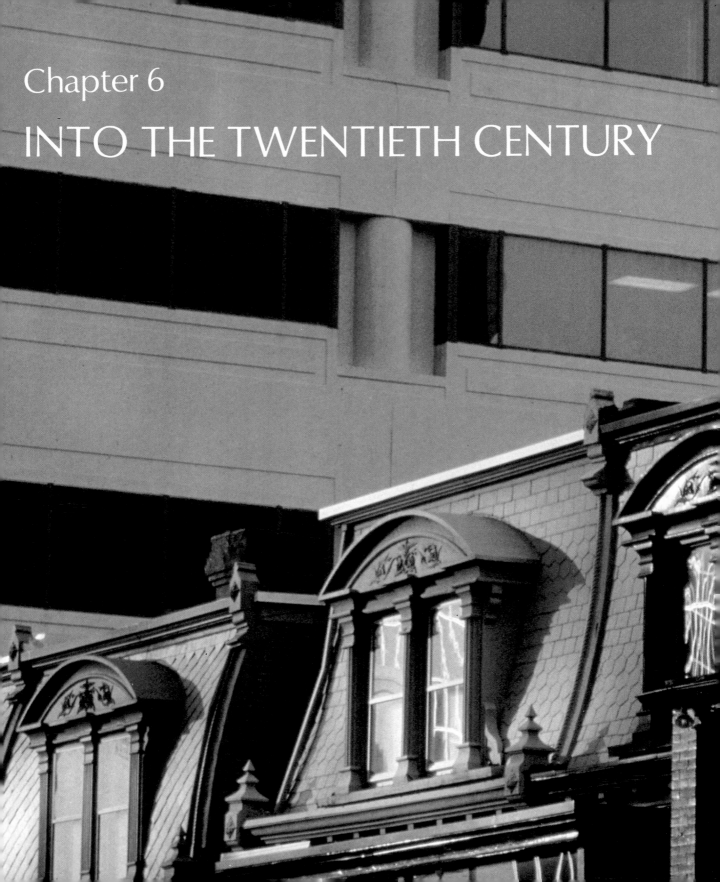

Chapter 6

INTO THE TWENTIETH CENTURY

INTO THE TWENTIETH CENTURY

In October 1938, the usually tranquil town of Seaford burst into a gala week-long celebration. Seaford had just been selected as the site for the world's first nylon factory. The sleepy farming community was about to leap into the industrial age.

The twentieth century heralded dramatic changes throughout the First State. Big business and modern agriculture combined to reshape the landscape of tiny Delaware.

DELAWARE'S FIRST FAMILY

In 1902, one hundred years after E. I. du Pont started making gunpowder on Brandywine Creek, three du Pont cousins took over the prosperous family business. Under the leadership of T. Coleman, Alfred I., and Pierre S. du Pont, the Du Pont Company gained a monopoly on powder manufacture in the United States. In 1907, the company was sued under the Sherman Anti-Trust Act, which forbade monopolies in business. The Du Pont Company was eventually forced to give up some of its operations. Much of the explosives business was taken over by two newly formed companies, the Atlas Powder Company and the Hercules Powder Company, both based in Wilmington.

The breakup of the powder monopoly stimulated the du Ponts to branch into new, untried territory. They invested in chemical plants that made lacquers, enamels, and dyes. Later, they began to

NYLON YARN

PURE DIAMINE

NYLON SALT

PURE ADIPIC ACID

CRUDE ?

NYLON POLYMER

After the breakup of the powder monopoly, the du Ponts turned to other ventures, including the manufacture of synthetic fabrics.

manufacture rayon and dacron, and set up research facilities to develop other synthetic fabrics. They supported factories that turned out automobiles.

Like King Midas in the ancient story, the du Ponts seemed to have a magical golden touch. Their enterprises boomed, their investments doubled and redoubled, and they amassed an extraordinary fortune. Perhaps it is ironic that the du Ponts, who grew wealthy by selling gunpowder, had a deep-seated social conscience. Happily for the people of Delaware, they channeled much of their wealth into projects that benefited their home state.

With a personal donation of $4 million, T. Coleman du Pont realized his dream of "building a monument one hundred miles high and laying it down the length of the state." In 1911, construction began on the Coleman du Pont Highway, the first divided highway in the nation. When it was completed in 1924, it

The children's hospital at Nemours, founded by the Alfred I. du Pont trust, provides a full range of pediatric health-care services. The family château (above) is open to the public.

extended from Wilmington to Delmar, on the Maryland border, giving Delaware easy access to Philadelphia and other northern cities.

Pierre S. du Pont directed his efforts toward improving education in Delaware. Early in the twentieth century, half the schools in the state were open less than seven months a year. Neither schools nor teachers had to meet certification standards. The school system was strictly segregated by race, and the black schools were far inferior to those for white children. While white schools received state funds, black schools were supported by a special property tax levied on black families only. In 1917, a Rockefeller Foundation commission studied Delaware's school system and concluded, "Delaware buys a low and cheap brand of education. Probably not more than seven other states spend so little."

Spurred on by the Rockefeller report, Pierre du Pont and a group of concerned citizens worked tirelessly to build a modern system of education. They established certification requirements for teachers and merged many one-room school districts to create better-equipped consolidated schools. Though the school system remained segregated, du Pont's group improved schools for black children as well as those for whites. Pierre du Pont personally paid for the construction of eighty-seven new schools to serve the black community.

Pierre du Pont was also a generous benefactor of the University of Delaware at Newark. Between 1914 and 1920, he gave the university more than $1 million, most of it used for new buildings. Fond of extravagant gestures, du Pont once arranged for a private train to take the school's entire faculty and student body to Wilmington for an evening at the theater.

The third of the du Pont cousins, Alfred I., was deeply concerned with the poor and the sick. In 1933, he persuaded the legislature to open a home and hospital for the indigent, the State Welfare Home at Smyrna. In his will, du Pont left a 300-acre (121-hectare) estate at Nemours to be used for the treatment of children who had polio or other disabling diseases. Shortly before his death in 1935, he wrote, "It has been my firm conviction throughout life that it is the duty of everyone in the world to do what is within his power to alleviate human suffering."

DELAWARE IN TWO WORLD WARS

About ten thousand Delawareans served in the armed forces in 1917 and 1918, when the United States was involved in World War I. Delaware troops comprised the bulk of the 59th Pioneer Infantry, which fought on the front lines in France.

Delaware's industries also made a major contribution to the war effort. Shipyards on the Christina River turned out naval vessels. The Du Pont Company manufactured about 40 percent of the gunpowder used by the Allies. More powder came from the newer Hercules and Atlas companies.

Agriculture boomed in Delaware in the years after World War I. Sussex County became one of the richest farming counties in the eastern United States. In 1923, Mrs. Wilmer Steele of Ocean View began raising broilers (chickens between five and twelve weeks old) for shipment to the big cities. Within twenty years, Delaware had captured one-fourth of the nation's commercial broiler market.

The nation slid into a severe economic depression in the 1930s. No major banks failed in Delaware, but thousands of workers lost their jobs. After the election of 1932, the nation turned for help to the new Democratic president, Franklin Delano Roosevelt. Delaware was one of only five states that had voted for Republican Herbert Hoover.

Programs under Roosevelt's "New Deal" created hundreds of jobs in Delaware. The government paid people to plant trees, clear hiking trails, and help with mosquito control. Federal money also stimulated the arts in Delaware, enabling the establishment of a symphony orchestra in Wilmington.

When the United States entered World War II, factories reopened and workers were hired for round-the-clock shifts. During World War II, shipbuilding replaced powder manufacture as Delaware's leading war industry. The Dravo Corporation, which operated shipyards near Wilmington, launched 187 naval vessels, including 15 destroyer escorts. Hercules and Atlas continued to manufacture explosives, although by this time Du Pont no longer manufactured powder within the state.

Between World Wars I and II, Delaware captured one-fourth of the nation's commercial broiler market.

However, the Du Pont Company did manufacture many other products necessary to the war effort, including nylon used in making parachutes. The Bancroft Cotton Mill in Wilmington made cloth for uniforms.

About one of every ten Delawareans served in the armed forces during World War II. Fighter pilots underwent training at Dover Municipal Airport. New Castle County Airport became a major dispatch point for troops heading to Asia or Europe. When the war was over at last, New Castle was the place where some fifteen thousand returning GIs first touched American soil.

CHANGES AND CHALLENGES

By 1945, Delaware had evolved a perplexingly inconsistent pattern of racial segregation. The races were kept rigidly apart in public schools, restaurants, and theaters. Yet public libraries and

When the frustrations of Wilmington's black community exploded in the summer of 1967, there were riots in the streets.

many churches were open to blacks and whites alike. The state maintained segregated reform schools for girls, while boys who got into trouble were sent to a single integrated facility.

In 1950, blacks for the first time were permitted unrestricted admission to the University of Delaware. A 1952 decision by the Delaware chancery court held that segregated black schools were inherently inferior to schools for white students, and the first public high schools in the state became integrated. This Delaware decision was cited two years later by the United States Supreme Court in the historic *Brown vs. Board of Education of Topeka* case.

School desegregation proceeded smoothly in New Castle County. In Kent and Sussex counties, however, change met with greater resistance. In 1955, the Milford Board of Education canceled a football game with Dover because one player on the Dover team was black. Statewide integration was not achieved until the early 1960s.

Delaware's population skyrocketed between 1950 and 1970. During the 1950s, it rose more than 40 percent, tapering to a 22 percent increase in the 1960s. No other eastern state except

Florida experienced such dramatic growth. Most of the newcomers were migrants from nearby states and were chiefly of European descent. In addition, some Chinese, Japanese, Filipino, and Puerto Rican families began to settle in the state, especially around Wilmington.

During the postwar years, farming families from Kent and Sussex counties began to leave the land. Many of them moved to Wilmington in search of jobs in industry. The farmers who remained took a more businesslike, scientific approach to agriculture. The broiler industry expanded, while other crops, such as strawberries, became less important. Farmers depended heavily on migrant laborers, many of them Hispanic.

As the population of New Castle County swelled, more and more factories and corporate offices moved to the suburbs around Wilmington. Families that could afford to move also left the city. Most of the people who abandoned Wilmington were middle-class whites. Few high-paying jobs were open to blacks. Most black families in Wilmington were unable to afford suburban homes.

The frustrations of Wilmington's black community exploded in July 1967. Riots in the streets left seven people wounded and led to 250 arrests. Months later, in April 1968, the assassination of black leader Reverend Martin Luther King, Jr., triggered a renewed outbreak of violence. To prevent further harm to property and to human lives, Governor Charles L. Terry called on the National Guard to patrol the city's black neighborhoods.

To the dismay of many Wilmington residents, however, the governor kept the troops on duty long after order was restored. The presence of the National Guard became a highly controversial issue and contributed to Governor Terry's defeat when he ran for reelection. His successor, Russell Peterson, dismissed the troops in January 1969.

During the 1970s and 1980s, Delaware launched many innovative programs to revitalize Wilmington and enhance opportunities for its low-income residents. In 1973, Wilmington pioneered an experimental "urban homesteading" project. Families were given crumbling, unoccupied houses free of charge, on condition that they make the necessary repairs. The program proved so successful that it was later adopted by the federal government and used in many other cities across the nation.

Elected for two terms beginning in 1985, Republican governor Michael Castle championed a series of statewide child-development programs and worked to revamp Delaware's welfare system. He trimmed the bureaucracy in state government and helped to bring the unemployment rate below 3 percent.

As campaigning heated up for the 1988 presidential race, Americans were introduced to two hopeful candidates from Delaware—Pierre "Pete" du Pont IV and Joseph Biden. As governor between 1977 and 1985, du Pont, a Republican, had cut state taxes and encouraged out-of-state banks to set up headquarters in Delaware. Democrat Joseph Biden, Delaware's junior United States senator, had played a key role on the Senate Judiciary Committee. Neither of these candidates survived the early stages of the campaign. But their visibility helped to bring the First State into the spotlight.

In addition to attracting out-of-state banks, Delaware has put out the welcome mat for businesses of all kinds. Generous tax breaks and a series of procorporation court decisions dating as far back as 1899 have created a favorable climate for companies that wish to set up corporate headquarters. By 1989, about half of America's Fortune 500 companies were incorporated in Delaware.

The latter half of the twentieth century brought a tremendous surge in Delaware's tourist industry. On sizzling summer days,

Delaware Republican Pierre ''Pete'' du Pont IV (left) and Democrat Joseph Biden (right) campaigned unsuccessfully for their party's 1988 nomination for president.

families from Philadelphia, Baltimore, and the Washington, D.C., area flock to Delaware's resorts along the Atlantic Coast. Rehoboth Beach became so popular with government workers that it is sometimes called the ''Nation's Summer Capital.''

In the summer of 1989, Walt Disney Studios released *The Dead Poets' Society*, a motion picture about boarding-school life. Filmed at St. Andrews School near Middletown, *The Dead Poets' Society* was the first full-length movie ever shot in Delaware. Pointing out the range of their state's scenic attractions, Delaware promoters are convinced that this film will not be the last made in Delaware. ''We have beaches, swamplands, rivers, a port, a canal, a bay, a ferry, marinas, and a rustic fishing village,'' states Dr. Frankie Miller of the Delaware Development Office. ''We have old farmhouses, Georgian or Victorian buildings, a colonial town.''

With a growing sense of pride, Delawareans have come to realize that their diminutive state has a great deal to offer—to business, to tourists, even to filmmakers. As the century draws to a close, Delaware looks toward a promising future.

Chapter 7

GOVERNMENT AND THE ECONOMY

GOVERNMENT AND THE ECONOMY

GOVERNMENT

Delaware is divided into three counties: New Castle, Kent, and Sussex. The counties are subdivided into "hundreds." Delaware is the only state that still uses the old English term hundred to designate a land zone. Like a township in some other states, a hundred may include one or more towns and their surrounding rural areas.

Delaware's state constitution was framed in 1897 and has been amended, or changed, many times. Amendments to the constitution may be passed by a two-thirds vote in two successive sessions of the General Assembly or by a special constitutional convention. Delaware is the only state that can amend its constitution without the direct approval of the voters.

Like the United States Constitution, Delaware's constitution divides state government into three branches: the legislative, the executive, and the judicial. The legislative branch passes and repeals laws; the executive branch ensures that the laws are carried out; and the judicial branch interprets the laws.

Delaware's legislature, the General Assembly, consists of an upper house, or senate, and a lower house, or house of representatives. The twenty-one state senators are elected to four-year terms. The forty-one members of the house of representatives serve two-year terms. Regular sessions of the General Assembly

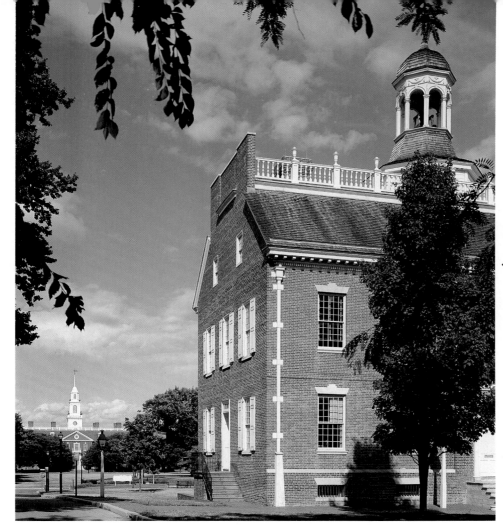

Dover's Old State House (foreground), built in 1792, is the second-oldest state capitol in continuous use. The state legislature meets in Legislative Hall (background).

open on the second Tuesday in January and do not extend beyond June 30. The executive branch of Delaware's state government is headed by the governor, who may be elected to two consecutive four-year terms. Other elected officials in the executive branch include the lieutenant governor, attorney general, insurance commissioner, state treasurer, and auditor of accounts. The governor appoints a secretary of state and the heads of many state departments, as well as judges and members of the state board of education.

Each of Delaware's counties has a family court and a court of common pleas. The superior court rotates on a regular basis from

The chamber of the state house of representatives

one county to another. Four associate justices and one chief justice sit on the bench of the supreme court, which is located in Dover, the state capital. Delaware also maintains an active court of chancery, which is a court of equity that often interprets corporate law.

Some laws dating back to colonial times still remain on the books in Delaware today. Delaware is the only state in which public whipping is still legal as a sentence for persons convicted of crimes. "Old Susan," as the whipping post was once called, was last used in the state in 1952.

About 50 percent of Delaware's revenue comes from taxes on income, gasoline, cigarettes, and utilities. Corporate taxes are very low in Delaware—one of the reasons so many companies choose to incorporate in the First State. Federal grants provide about one-fifth of the revenue in the state budget.

Memorial Hall, University of Delaware

EDUCATION

The largest single item in Delaware's budget is education.
According to state law, all children from the ages of five through
fifteen must attend school. About sixty-three thousand students
attend public elementary schools in Delaware, and some thirty
thousand are enrolled in public high schools. An additional
twenty-three thousand students attend private or parochial
schools.

The University of Delaware, in Newark, is the largest institution
of higher learning in the state. The university, which began in
1834 as Newark Academy, was housed in a building known today
as Old College Hall. Newark Academy evolved into Newark
College and finally became the University of Delaware in 1921.
About fourteen thousand undergraduate and graduate students

Students at Delaware State College, about 1900

attend the university, which offers degrees in nursing, business, oceanography, urban affairs, engineering, and many other fields of study.

Delaware State College, in Dover, was founded in 1891 as a college for black men and women. White women could not attend college in Delaware until Newark College became coeducational in 1914.

Among Delaware's other colleges and universities are Goldey Beacom College, in Wilmington; Wesley College, in Dover; Wilmington College, in New Castle; and Brandywine College of Widener University, in Wilmington.

TRANSPORTATION AND COMMUNICATION

Cars and trucks roll across Delaware along nearly 5,300 miles (8,529 kilometers) of paved roads and highways. The Coleman

The Lewes and Reheboth Canal (above) connects Lewes and Reheboth Bay.

du Pont Highway (U.S. 13) has been the state's chief artery for traffic since its completion in 1924. About 300 miles (483 kilometers) of railroad track crisscross the state, which is served by four freight lines. Wilmington is the only city in Delaware that still enjoys passenger service.

Delaware has fifteen public and private airfields. The largest of these is the Greater Wilmington Airport, located outside New Castle. The Chesapeake and Delaware Canal, which crosses the state south of New Castle, saves ships a 285-mile (459-kilometer) journey around the Delmarva Peninsula on their way from Baltimore to the Atlantic Ocean. The Lewes and Rehoboth Canal provides a shortcut for ships past the barrier islands along the Atlantic Coast.

Delaware has at least fifteen weekly newspapers and two dailies: the *Delaware State News*, of Dover, and the *Morning News*, published in Wilmington. The state's first radio station, WDEL,

The Wilmington train station serves the only city in Delaware that still enjoys passenger service.

went on the air in Wilmington in 1922. Television came to the state in 1949. Today Delaware has twenty radio stations and an educational television channel.

AGRICULTURE

About 50 percent of Delaware's land area is devoted to farming. But agriculture comprises only 1 percent of the gross state product (GSP) — the total value of goods and services produced in the state within a given year. Delaware has some thirty-five hundred farms, which average 185 acres (75 hectares) in size.

Nearly 60 percent of Delaware's farm income is generated by the broiler-chicken industry, which is concentrated in Sussex County. Dairy cows graze in Kent and southern New Castle counties.

Though the broiler-chicken industry generates most of Delaware's farm income, dairy products, vegetables, and fruit are also produced.

Corn and soybeans are the leading field crops grown in Delaware. The bulk of this grain is used as feed for the state's 200 million chickens. In the late 1980s, some Delaware farmers began to experiment with raising such exotic vegetables as truffles, shallots, and Chinese cabbage, which earn a high profit per acre.

MANUFACTURING

Manufacturing accounts for about 34 percent of Delaware's GSP. Only in Michigan is manufacturing a larger element in the state economy. Delaware is one of the nation's leading states in chemical research. The Center for Composite Materials at the University of Delaware, in Newark, is the world's chief laboratory for the development of composite substances. Composites are

Chemical research (left) and food processing (right) generate a large portion of Delaware's gross state product.

made by blending existing materials such as glass, polyesters, and plastics to form new materials that can withstand extreme heat and stress in space travel. Companies including Du Pont, Hercules, and Imperial Chemicals Industry (ICI) sponsor extensive research and manufacture paints, plastics, synthetic fabrics, and a host of other chemical products.

Food processing is the second-most important manufacturing industry in Delaware. Milford is the hub of the poultry-processing business. Canneries operate in Wilmington, and Sussex County is famous for its pickles.

Automobile assembly plants operate at Newark and Newport. Other factories in the state make paper, rubber products, and plastic products.

Delaware's service industries—including finance, insurance, and trade—are concentrated in and around Wilmington (above).

SERVICE INDUSTRIES

The service industries comprise the largest portion of Delaware's economy, accounting for 59 percent of the GSP. Instead of producing manufactured goods, people employed in the service industries provide services to individuals or groups. Beauticians, doctors, waitresses, lawyers, and auto mechanics are among the thousands of people who work in service industries.

Delaware's service industries are concentrated in and around Wilmington, the heart of finance, insurance, and trade in the state. Home base to some 173,000 corporations, large and small, Delaware has thousands of workers involved in sales and administration. Although they maintain offices in Delaware, most of these companies conduct the greater part of their operations in other states.

Chapter 8

ARTS AND RECREATION

ARTS AND RECREATION

Native Delawareans and those who moved to the state later in life have made lasting contributions to American literature, painting, and the performing arts. Delaware also offers generous recreational opportunities for lovers of sports of all kinds.

LITERATURE

Delaware's foremost statesman of the Revolutionary War era was John Dickinson, who grew up near Dover. In 1801, Dickinson published *Political Writings*, a collection of the petitions, declarations, and letters he had composed during the preceding quarter century. The collection included Dickinson's appeals to the king of England issued from the Continental Congress and a series of letters in support of the United States Constitution.

Robert Montgomery Bird, of New Castle, was a doctor who claimed that he turned to writing plays because he hated charging his patients. His plays *The Broker of Bogota* and *The Gladiator* were highly successful during his lifetime. He is also remembered for his novel *Hawks of Hawk Hollow*, which appeared in 1835.

Another physician who turned to writing was John Lofland of Milford. Much of his poetry was inspired by the scenery of Delaware, especially of the Brandywine Valley. Lofland's first book of poems, *Harp of Delaware*, was published in 1828, and his collected works appeared in 1848. Writing as the "Milford Bard," Lofland ran a series of newspaper advertisements offering to write, for a fee, lectures, love letters, songs, acrostics, or

This Howard Pyle illustration of the Battle of Germantown appeared in *Scribners Magazine* in June 1898.

inscriptions for tombs. Despite his many enterprises, Lofland died in poverty, an alcoholic and an opium addict. He is buried in Wilmington in an unmarked grave.

Born in Georgetown, George Alfred Townsend documented the events of the Civil War in gripping newspaper accounts, which he published under the pen name "Gath." In 1880, he published *Tales of the Chesapeake*, a collection of folktales gathered in Delaware and Maryland. Townsend's 1884 novel *The Entailed Hat* tells the story of Patty Cannon, who captured hundreds of free black people and sold them into slavery.

Wilmington was home to writer, teacher, and illustrator Howard Pyle for most of his life. Many of Pyle's children's books are considered classics today. Pyle wrote and illustrated stories about knights, pirates, and noblemen, and his books are packed with adventure. His works include *The Merrie Adventures of Robin Hood*, *The Story of King Arthur and His Knights*, *Otto of the Silver Hand*, *The Ghost of Captain Brand*, and *The Price of Blood*.

The world-famous "muckraker" Upton Sinclair moved to the town of Arden in 1911 and lived there for several years. Sinclair used fiction to make the public aware of social injustices. His novel *The Jungle*, published in 1906, exposed the horrors of Chicago's meat-packing industry.

Essayist Henry Seidel Canby, born in Wilmington, founded the highly acclaimed magazine *Saturday Review of Literature* in 1924. His work *The Age of Confidence* examines Wilmington society as an example of American life. Anne Parish's 1925 novel *The Perennial Bachelor*, modeling its characters on people she knew in Claymont, takes a more humorous view of Delaware life.

Two important twentieth-century novelists who are not usually associated with Delaware have connections to the First State. Though most of his works are set in Boston, John P. Marquand was born in Wilmington. F. Scott Fitzgerald, a member of the "Lost Generation" of writers who worked in Paris in the early 1920s, lived and partied extravagantly in Wilmington from 1927 to 1929.

ART

Colonial Delaware nurtured many fine artisans whose works are prized by collectors today. Cabinetmakers, clock makers, coach makers, and silversmiths elevated their trades to an art form. Itinerant artists carried bundles of canvases from farm to farm, painting family portraits.

The first Delaware portrait painter to win wide recognition was Swedish immigrant Gustavus Hesselius. He is also regarded as the first organ maker in the colonies. His son, John Hesselius, became a painter as well and taught noted Philadelphia artist Charles Willson Peale.

Frank Schoonover's *Trapper with Christmas Tree* **and J. D. Chalfant's** *Clockmaker* **are representative of the work of these Delaware artists.**

Two nineteenth-century painters depicted charming scenes of Delaware life. The landscape paintings of Henry Lea Tatnall were inspired by the natural beauty of the Brandywine Valley. J. D. Chalfant, who spent most of his life in Newport, created detailed scenes of Delawareans at work and at play.

In 1900, writer and illustrator Howard Pyle opened a school of art in Wilmington. He offered classes free of charge to young artists of exceptional talent. One of Pyle's students was Frank Schoonover, a landscape artist and illustrator. Some of his best-known paintings depict Canadian trappers and Indians. Pyle's most famous pupil was Newell Convers (N. C.) Wyeth, a muralist and illustrator. N. C. Wyeth's son Andrew is one of America's most popular twentieth-century painters.

By the latter half of the century, Delaware artists turned to new subjects and forms of expression. The works of Joe Moss, who

Sailboat racing is a popular summertime sport in Delaware waters.

teaches art at the University of Delaware, appeal to both the eye
and the ear. The graceful curves of his large steel sculptures echo
footsteps, clapping hands, and even whispered words. One of
Moss's pieces stands outside the Delaware Art Museum and is
regarded as its logo. America's urban landscape comes to life in
the paintings of Ed Loper. Born in Wilmington, Loper captures the
spirit of survival of black people in the inner city.

PERFORMING ARTS

Live music and theater are concentrated in Wilmington. The
Delaware Symphony performs at Wilmington's Grand Opera
House, which was built in 1871 as a Masonic Temple. The
symphony has been active since the 1930s, when it was
established with funds from President Roosevelt's New Deal.
Performing in North Wilmington, the Wilmington Drama
League is the state's oldest community theater. The Playhouse

Theater offers musicals, comedies, and dramas at the Du Pont Building in Wilmington's downtown business district. The Delaware Theater Company puts on classics and contemporary plays at a little theater near the Christina River. In addition, the University of Delaware hosts a variety of plays and concerts each year in Newark.

SPORTS AND RECREATION

Delaware has never had a professional baseball, football, or basketball team. Most sports fans in the First State root for teams from Philadelphia or Baltimore. Devotees of college football cheer for the University of Delaware's Blue Hens.

Although Delaware has never had a professional baseball team of its own, it has produced some outstanding players. One of the early greats of baseball history was John Joseph "Sadie" McMahon of Rising Sun, a star with the Baltimore Orioles in the 1890s. Victor Willis, another early star, won 247 games with the Boston Braves, the Pittsburgh Pirates, and the St. Louis Cardinals. Julius "Judy" Johnson, who grew up in Wilmington, starred in the Negro League. As a scout for the Milwaukee Braves and the Philadelphia Phillies, he helped talented black players enter the major leagues.

During the summer months, boatloads of sports fishermen set out each morning from Lewes. The offshore waters yield such prizes as white marlin, yellowfin tuna, Atlantic mackerel, and bluefish. One popular game fish, the weakfish, is so named because its mouth tears easily when it is hooked, and it must be lifted into the boat with a net. Along Delaware Bay, crabbing and clamming provide family fun. Controlled hunting is permitted in Bombay Hook and Prime Hook national wildlife refuges.

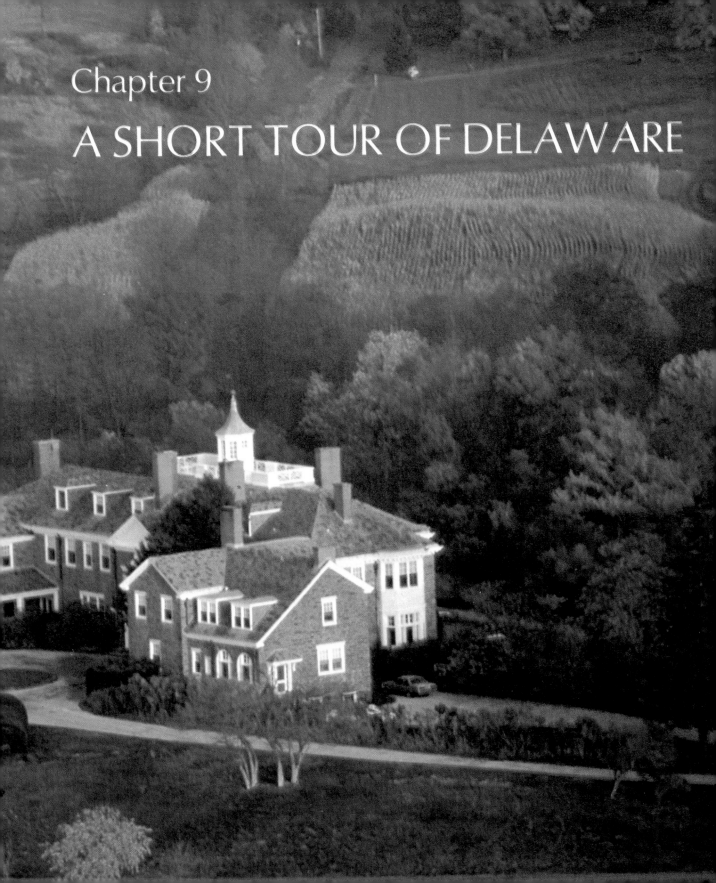

Chapter 9
A SHORT TOUR OF DELAWARE

A SHORT TOUR OF DELAWARE

Tourism plays a major role in Delaware's economy. At first, out-of-staters are usually lured by Delaware's sparkling beaches. But the First State also has charming small towns, historic homes, and fascinating museums, as well as ten state parks and four state forests. Curious visitors quickly discover that Delaware has many surprises in store.

NEW CASTLE COUNTY

Located at the northern tip of the state, New Castle is both the smallest and the most densely populated of Delaware's three counties. It is the hub of business and industry in the state.

Three miles (5 kilometers) from the point where Delaware, Maryland, and Pennsylvania meet stands the lively university town of Newark. During colonial times, Newark was a thriving crossroads trade center, where travelers and merchants from the three states exchanged goods and swapped news. Generously endowed by the du Pont family, the University of Delaware has an outstanding science curriculum and conducts extensive research in chemistry. Just northwest of Newark, the Walter S. Carpenter, Jr., State Park offers canoeing, horseback riding, hiking, and camping.

Wilmington, on the banks of the Christina River, is Delaware's largest city and the state's main cultural center. At the heart of

The Wilmington Men's Club, on Market Street

Wilmington lies Rodney Square, a small park graced by a mounted statue of Caesar Rodney. The statue commemorates Rodney's historic 1776 ride. The high-rise Du Pont Building (known locally as "the Building") overlooks the park. The Building houses the Du Pont Company's headquarters, the Playhouse Theater, the Hotel du Pont, and the offices of many leading banks and law firms.

Old Town Hall, in downtown Wilmington, now houses the Historical Society of Delaware. The society sponsors changing exhibits on Delaware's history, arts, and crafts. Displays include furniture, silver, Early American toys, and a remarkably elaborate Victorian dollhouse. The Historical Society also maintains an extensive library, with a wealth of newspapers, maps, manuscripts, photographs, and books about Delaware's past.

The statue of Caesar Rodney, at Rodney Square in Wilmington

The Market Street Mall is an inviting strip of restaurants and shops, flanked by some of Wilmington's finest buildings. Across Market Street Mall from Old Town Hall is Willingtown Square. The square was created in 1976, when four eighteenth-century houses were moved there to save them from demolition. The houses are now used as office buildings.

Constructed in 1698, Wilmington's Old Swedes Church is the oldest church in the United States still in use. The church contains many reminders of Delaware's early Swedish settlers, including a 1713 chest in which cash and valuables were once locked away. Several graves, among them those of five children, lie beneath the church's brick floor. Near the church is the Kalmar Nyckel Museum and Shipyard, a living-history exhibit that documents the beginning history of the first Swedish settlement.

The Delaware Art Museum, just west of Wilmington, opened in

The grounds of the Hagley Museum on Brandywine Creek

1912 with a collection of works by illustrator Howard Pyle. The museum has expanded to include paintings by such American masters as Benjamin West, Winslow Homer, and George Inness. The museum's Bancroft Collection is the nation's most outstanding group of works by the nineteenth-century British painters known as the Pre-Raphaelites.

The Hagley Museum and Eleutherian Mills stand on the original site where E. I. du Pont began his powder mill in 1802. The museum traces the history of industry in America and shows how nineteenth-century mill workers lived. Visitors can see pieces of early industrial machinery in action, including a giant waterwheel.

One of the finest museums in Delaware is the Henry Francis du Pont Winterthur Museum and Gardens, northwest of Wilmington. The nine-story museum houses more than eighty thousand

The Henry Francis
du Pont Winterthur
Museum and Gardens,
northwest of
Wilmington (right),
is one of the finest
museums in Delaware.
The centerpiece of
Nemours, the
Alfred I. du Pont
estate northeast of
Wilmington (below),
is a Louis XVI-style
château and French
gardens that are
open to the public.
The George Read II
House, in New Castle
(below right), has
been fully restored.

examples of American decorative arts and crafts spanning the period from 1640 to 1860. Exhibits include whole rooms displaying furniture, ceramics, textiles, metalwork, paintings, and prints. An open-air tram takes visitors through the formal gardens that surround the museum building.

Another gift from the du Pont family is Bellevue State Park, the former estate of William H. du Pont, Jr. The centerpiece of the 271-acre (110-hectare) park is Bellevue Hall, a forty-nine-room Gothic mansion surrounded by magnificent gardens, tennis courts, a riding stable, and a golf course.

The town of Arden, north of Wilmington, was founded in 1900 as a "single-tax" community. Its residents were taxed only according to the value of their undeveloped land, regardless of any improvements they chose to make. Early in the century, Arden attracted many Socialists and even a few anarchists (persons who wish to do away with all forms of government). In 1911, Arden became home to writer Upton Sinclair.

New Castle, on the Delaware River, served as Delaware's colonial capital. The spire of the Old Court House acted as a compass point for the surveyors who marked Delaware's curved northern boundary. New Castle's old section still has many cobblestone streets. The George Read II House was built by the son of George Read, one of Delaware's signers of the Declaration of Independence. The house has been fully restored, with elaborate carved woodwork, gilded fanlights, and silver door handles. Another interesting restored home is the Old Dutch House, believed to be the oldest brick dwelling in Delaware. The Old Dutch House is considered to be the finest example of Dutch colonial architecture in the state.

Ships passing through the C & D Canal enter the Delaware River at Delaware City. During the summer months, a ferry

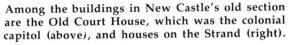
Among the buildings in New Castle's old section are the Old Court House, which was the colonial capitol (above), and houses on the Strand (right).

shuttles visitors back and forth from Delaware City to Pea Patch Island, site of the once-notorious Civil War prison. The octagonal Fort Delaware is still standing. Visitors can enter the great iron gates, cross the parade grounds, and explore the underground cells where many captives were shut away. The marshlands at the northern end of Pea Patch Island shelter a large and noisy colony of herons and egrets.

Odessa is noted for many carefully preserved vintage houses. The Corbit-Sharp House displays many of the furnishings that belonged to its original owner, William Corbit. The Wilson-Warner House is an antique-lover's delight, with furniture and kitchen implements of the early nineteenth century.

KENT COUNTY

Rural Kent County is a patchwork of farmers' fields, dotted with some of the state's most delightful small towns. Smyrna is an

The interior of the Old State House,
in the Old Dover Historic District

excellent place to view a variety of architectural styles dating as
far back as the Revolutionary War. Along Delaware Bay east of
Smyrna, some 15,000 acres (6,070 hectares) of wetlands are
protected within the Bombay Hook National Wildlife Refuge. This
sanctuary is a breeding site for thousands of ducks, Canada geese,
herons, and other waterfowl. Inside the refuge stands Allee
House, one of Delaware's most prized historic homes.

The Old Dover Historic District, in downtown Dover, preserves
many of the state capital's dignified early buildings. The Old State
House is the second-oldest state capitol in continuous use. The
Hall of Records displays many priceless documents that shaped
the state's history, including the charter of 1682 that granted the
Lower Counties to William Penn. In the cemetery of Christ
Episcopal Church (built in 1734) stands a monument to Caesar
Rodney. The stately brick Delaware Supreme Court building

The small park in Dover called The Green

overlooks a small square park called The Green. On The Green in 1776, Delawareans heard a reading of the Declaration of Independence. The reading inspired a crowd to burn a portrait of the British king, George III.

Nearby, at Constitution Park, stands a unique monument to Delaware's role in ratifying the Constitution. The entire document is inscribed on a 4-foot (1-meter) stone cube. Atop the cube rests a 12-foot (4-meter) quill pen, cast in bronze.

The Delaware State Museum, in Dover, traces the history of the First State through photographs, newspaper clippings, letters, and exhibits of early crafts. One gallery features century-old shops. The museum also has a large collection of early phonographs and recordings. The Delaware Agricultural Museum documents two hundred years of farm life and displays a fine collection of tractors and other farming machinery.

The United States Constitution is inscribed on a stone cube in Dover's Constitution Park.

Among Dover's many historic houses is Woodburn, built in 1791. It once served as a station on the Underground Railroad. Woodburn has been the official home of the state governor since 1966. Rose Cottage was the home of J. A. Fulton, an authority on peaches, who fostered the growing of peaches in Delaware after the Civil War. Cannon House, built in 1862, was the home of astronomer Annie Jump Cannon.

The John Dickinson Plantation, south of Dover, has been fully restored to its early nineteenth-century appearance. The plantation was the home of John Dickinson, known as the "Penman of the American Revolution."

Many picturesque small towns lie in the southern part of Kent County. Camden, which began as a Quaker settlement, has several fine homes of the Federal period. To the west lies Wyoming, once a thriving railroad town.

The *C-5 Galaxy*, on exhibit at Dover Air Force Base, is the largest cargo plane in the western world.

Anyone with an interest in planes will want to visit the Historical Center of Dover Air Force Base. Among the aircraft on exhibit is the *C-5 Galaxy*, the largest cargo plane in the western world. The collection also includes the *C-45*, *C-47*, and *C-54*.

During the summer, life in Bowers revolves around fishing, with boats setting out each morning to net the daily catch. The history of shipbuilding, sailing, and fishing in Delaware comes to life at the Bowers Beach Maritime Museum.

Frederica is known as the "Cradle of Methodism in America." At Barratt's Chapel in 1784, two renowned Methodist leaders from England—Francis Asbury and Thomas Coke—met to organize the Methodist Episcopal Church of America.

Each July, Harrington hosts the Delaware State Fair. Farmers enter their poultry, goats, and cows in competitions, while children sample delicious homemade jams, breads, and cakes. Music, rides, and games of chance entertain the whole family.

Bethany Beach is a resort town on Delaware's barrier reef.

SUSSEX COUNTY

Enormous modern chicken coops sprout along the roads of Sussex County, heart of Delaware's broiler-chicken industry. Like Kent County, Sussex is sprinkled with small towns that recall the state's long history and are rich in Delaware lore. Milford, on the Mispillion River, honors Delaware's state fish at its annual Weakfish Tournament. Many of the homes in Milford were built in the nineteenth century. George Beswick Hynson, who composed the state song, is buried here.

The Thursday after Election Day is Return Day in Georgetown. Dressed in colonial costumes, winning and losing candidates ride together through the streets in one car, cheered by the voters of both parties. While many Delaware towns have a central square, Georgetown was laid out in 1791 around a circular green.

The Nanticoke Indian Powwow is held every September in Millsboro.

Seaford, on the Nanticoke River near the Maryland border, is known as the "Nylon Capital of the World." About twenty-four hundred men and women work in the nylon plant, which opened here in 1939. Despite its importance as a factory center, Seaford retains the peaceful atmosphere of a country town, with handsome frame houses set along shaded streets. The Ross Mansion, built in 1850, was the home of Delaware governor William Henry Harrison Ross. Trap Pond State Park, near Laurel, encompasses a portion of the Pocomoke Swamp, which once sprawled over 50,000 acres (20,234 hectares) of land on Delaware's southern border. In the past, the swamp was the scene of a series of spectacular fires, part of its natural cycle of destruction and renewal. The flames of a great blaze in 1787 lit up the sky 70 miles (113 kilometers) away. The last major swamp fire occurred in 1930.

The Fenwick Island Lighthouse was built in 1857.

Every September, members of the Nanticoke Indian tribe invite the public to join them in two days of dance and feasting at the Nanticoke Indian Powwow in Millsboro. Millsboro's Nanticoke Museum features stone weapons and implements and other artifacts of Delaware's Native American people.

Sussex County's Atlantic Coast is ragged with bays, inlets, and brackish tidal rivers. Fenwick Island, at the Maryland boundary, remains in a wild state, much as it must have looked when Henry Hudson sailed up the coast in 1609. The easternmost marking stone of Mason and Dixon's Line is still in place.

Farther north, the beaches of Delaware's great barrier reef are playgrounds for vacationers. Bethany Beach caters to families with children. On sizzling afternoons, sand castles wait for the tide to sweep them away, and barefoot boys and girls scamper along the old-fashioned boardwalk, chewing saltwater taffy.

The name *Rehoboth* comes from a Biblical word meaning "room enough" and recalls the days when the air rang with hymns from Methodist camp meetings at Rehoboth Beach. Today, the town is so popular with government workers from Washington that it is often called the "Nation's Summer Capital." While Bethany Beach is relatively sedate, Rehoboth Beach throbs to the beat of discotheques at night.

Delaware Seashore State Park on Rehoboth Bay boasts nearly 7 miles (11 kilometers) of beaches for swimming and sunbathing. Sailboats glide along the bay, and anglers battle with bluefish, striped bass, and sea trout. Blue crabs can be caught in wire cages baited with chunks of meat. Clam diggers search out tasty shellfish hidden beneath the sand.

Atlantic breakers rake the southern shore of Cape Henlopen, but the northern side is washed by the gentle waves of Delaware Bay. Soaring, wind-sculpted sand dunes give Cape Henlopen an otherworldly appearance. One great pinnacle of sand, towering 80 feet (24 meters) into the air, is the tallest dune between Cape Hatteras and Cape Cod.

It has sometimes been said that the town of Lewes (pronounced "Lewis"), on Cape Henlopen, is to Delaware what Plymouth is to Massachusetts. Today, the Zwaanendael Museum commemorates the Dutch colony that was founded here in 1631, the first European settlement in Delaware. The people of Lewes are also proud of their town's resistance under British attack during the War of 1812. The Cannonball House Marine Museum is so named because a British cannonball is still lodged in its wall. From the drawbridge over the Lewes and Rehoboth Canal, a visitor can watch sailboats and chartered fishing craft heading out to sea. It is not hard to imagine the days when Lewes was the bustling fishing capital of the Delmarva Peninsula.

A lone man
fishes from
the jetty
at Indian
River Inlet.

Even in a brief tour, it is apparent that the people of Delaware treasure diversity. While Delaware encourages industry and agriculture, it also preserves the beauty of its woods and wetlands. In downtown Wilmington, eighteenth-century houses stand in the shadow of glass-and-steel high rises. Delawareans cherish their natural environment and respect their historic roots, yet they never forget their firm commitment to progress.

DECEMBER 7, 1787

FACTS AT A GLANCE

GENERAL INFORMATION

Statehood: December 7, 1787, first state to enter the Union

Origin of Name: Named for Sir Thomas West, Lord De La Warr

State Capital: Dover, capital since 1777

State Nicknames: ''First State,'' ''Diamond State,'' and ''Blue Hen State''

State Flag: Delaware's flag is colonial blue with the coat of arms on a buff-colored diamond. Below the diamond is the date of statehood. The coat of arms has a farmer and a rifleman flanking a shield that bears symbols of the state's agricultural resources. Those symbols are a sheaf of wheat, an ear of corn, and an ox. Above these symbols is a ship in full sail. Below the symbols is a banner with the state motto.

State Motto: ''Liberty and Independence''

State Bird: Blue hen chicken

State Flower: Peach blossom

State Tree: American holly

State Insect: Ladybug

State Colors: Colonial blue and buff

State Song: ''Our Delaware,'' music by George B. Hynson and words by Will M. S. Brown:

> Oh the hills of dear New Castle,
> And the smiling vales between,
> When the corn is all in tassel,
> And the meadow lands are green;
> Where the cattle crop the clover,
> And its breath is in the air,
> While the sun is shining over
> Our beloved Delaware.

The covered bridge over Red Clay Creek, Wood Dale

Chorus:

Oh, our Delaware!
Our beloved Delaware!
For the sun is shining over
Our beloved Delaware,
Oh! Our Delaware!
Our beloved Delaware!
Here's the loyal son that pledges,
Faith to good old Delaware.

Where the wheat fields break and billow,
In the peaceful land of Kent,
Where the toiler seeks his pillow,
With the blessings of content;
Where the bloom that tints the peaches,
Cheeks of merry maidens share,
And the woodland chorus preaches
A rejoicing Delaware.

(Chorus)

Dear old Sussex visions linger,
Of the holly and the pine,
Of Henlopen's Jeweled finger,
Flashing out across the brine;
Of the gardens and the hedges,
And the welcome waiting there,
For the loyal son that pledges
Faith to good old Delaware.

(Chorus)

From New Castle's rolling meadows,
Through the fair rich fields of Kent,
To the Sussex shores hear echoes,
Of the pledge we now present:
Liberty and Independence,
We will guard with loyal care,
And hold fast to freedom's presence,
In our home state Delaware.

(Chorus)

110

POPULATION

Population: 594,338, forty-seventh among the states (1980 census)

Population Density: 291 people per sq. mi. (112 people per km^2)

Population Distribution: 71 percent of the state's people live in cities and towns. Most Delawareans live in the northern city of Wilmington and nearby towns.

Wilmington	70,195
Newark	25,247
Dover	23,507
Elsmere	6,493
Milford	5,366
Seaford	5,256
New Castle	4,907
Lewes	2,197

(Population figures according to 1980 census)

Population Growth: Delaware's population has grown over the years. Although its small size has always kept it one of America's least populated states, Delaware is one of the most densely populated states. It has grown more rapidly than most other states and has nearly doubled its population since 1950, as more people move from the crowded cities of Philadelphia, Baltimore, and Washington, D.C.

Year	Population
1790	59,096
1800	64,273
1820	72,749
1840	78,085
1860	112,216
1880	146,608
1900	184,735
1920	223,003
1940	266,505
1950	318,085
1960	446,292
1970	548,104
1980	594,338

GEOGRAPHY

Borders: Delaware is bordered by Pennsylvania on the north and Maryland on the south and west. The border with Pennsylvania is the only border between two states that is formed by the arc of a perfect circle.

111

Highest Point: Elbright Road, in New Castle County, 442 ft. (135 m)

Lowest Point: Sea level

Greatest Distances: North to south—96 mi. (154 km)
                        East to west—39 mi. (63 km)

Area: 2,044 sq. mi. (5,294 km²)

Rank in Area Among the States: Forty-ninth

Rivers: The Delaware River, which gave its name to the state, forms part of the eastern boundary. It flows into Delaware Bay, an arm of the Atlantic Ocean. The state has many other smaller rivers. Gravelly Brook and Broad Creek join near the state's southwest boundary to form the Nanticoke River, which empties into Chesapeake Bay. The Chester and Choptank rivers, which also enter Chesapeake Bay, have their origins in Delaware. Smaller southern rivers—including the St. Jones, Broadkill, Murderkill, and Mispillion—flow into Delaware Bay. In the north, the Christina and Brandywine rivers meet at Wilmington, then feed into the Delaware. Other Delaware tributaries are the Smyrna and the Appoquinimink.

Lakes: Delaware has no large lakes. In fact, the entire state has only 75 sq. mi. (194 km²) of inland water, an area smaller than that of the largest lakes of most other states. Delaware's largest lake is Lums Pond, only 200 acres (81 hectares) in size. The state contains several man-made lakes and ponds.

Coasts: Delaware has 28 mi. (45 km) of coastline along the Atlantic Ocean. It has 381 mi. (613 km) of shoreline, counting the outer coast, offshore islands, bays, rivers, and creeks. The coastline extends from Cape Henlopen to the southern boundary at Fenwick Island. Rehoboth Bay, Indian River Bay, and Little Assawoman Bay, all in the southern part of the state, form many miles of this shoreline. A long sand reef separates these bays from the ocean.

Topography: Most of Delaware lies within the Atlantic Coastal Plain, a flat, low-lying area that seldom rises above 80 ft. (24 m). Slow, lazy-moving rivers amble through this plain on their way to the coast. The Great Pocomoke Swamp (also called Cypress Swamp), is a 30,000-acre (12,141-hectare) swampland that covers the southern part of the state.
North of the Christina River lies the Piedmont, a region of gently rolling hills and scenic, fertile valleys. This section contains Delaware's highest elevation, a point along Elbright Road near the Pennsylvania state line.

Climate: Its closeness to the Atlantic Ocean provides Delaware with a very humid climate. Summers can be very hot. Winters are usually mild because mountains in Pennsylvania deflect harsh winds from the northwest. Temperatures in Wilmington range from about 25° to 42° F. (-4° to 6° C) in January and 65° to 87° F. (18° to 31° C) in July. Lewes temperatures range from about 31° to 47° F. (-0.5° to 8° C) in January and 69° to 85° F. (21° to 29° C) in July. The state averages about 46 in. (117 cm) of precipitation each year.

Fall colors at Bombay Hook National Wildlife Refuge

NATURE

Trees: American hollies, hickories, beeches, black tupelos, pines, oaks, sassafrases, wild dogwoods, sweet gums, cypresses, white cedars, beach plums, maples, sycamores, walnuts, laurels, wild cherry trees

Wild Plants: Crocuses, violets, azaleas, honeysuckles, trumpet vines, Turk's-cap lilies, lady's slippers, morning glories, butterfly weeds, water lilies, buttonbushes, ferns, club mosses, Egyptian lotuses, orchids, swamp magnolias, hibiscuses, blueberries, cranberries

Birds: Blue herons, ducks, hawks, cardinals, Baltimore orioles, ruby-throated hummingbirds, sandpipers, snowy egrets, grackles, titmice, woodpeckers, teals, finches, blue jays

Animals: Deer, foxes, muskrats, minks, beavers, otters, rabbits, turtles, snakes

Fish and shellfish: Shad, sturgeons, rockfish, porgies, drumfish, bass, pickerels, bluegills, yellow perch, crappies, rainbow trout, blue trout, sea trout, menhaden, carp, catfish, weakfish, oysters, clams

GOVERNMENT

The first constitution of the First State was approved in 1776, the year of the Declaration of Independence. Two others were adopted in 1792 and 1831. The present state constitution, in effect since 1897, has been amended more than one hundred times. Amendments may be proposed by either the legislature or a constitutional convention. They become valid when approved by two-thirds of the members of both houses of the legislature, then reapproved by the next legislature following a general election. Delaware is the only state that does not require voter approval for constitutional amendments.

Delaware's government, like the federal government, consists of three branches. The legislature, called the General Assembly, is the state's law-making body. It contains a twenty-one-member senate and a forty-one-member house of representatives. Senators serve four-year terms and representatives serve two-year terms. Regular sessions begin each year in January and may not extend beyond June 30. The governor or leaders of either house may call for special sessions.

The executive branch, headed by the governor, is responsible for administering the law. Other important elected officials include the lieutenant governor, attorney general, insurance commissioner, state treasurer, and auditor of accounts. All are elected to four-year terms. The governor serves a four-year term and may be reelected only once. The governor appoints the secretary of state, the state board of education, and many other important officials.

Courts form the judicial branch. All judges are appointed by the governor with the approval of the senate. The state's highest court is the supreme court, which has a chief justice, chosen by the governor, and four associate justices. The superior court has eleven justices. Each county has a register's court and courts of common pleas, and Wilmington has a municipal court. Delaware also has a court of chancery, a court of equity that often interprets corporate law.

Number of Counties: 3

U.S. Representatives: 1

Electoral Votes: 3

Voting Qualifications: U.S. citizen, eighteen years of age, must reside in Delaware and register by the last day that books are open for registration.

EDUCATION

Ever since the time of the earliest Swedish and Dutch colonists, Delaware has provided some sort of education for many of its residents. For the most part, private religious groups supported the schools. The Quakers built Friends School in Wilmington, the oldest school in the state. Newark Academy, which later became the University of Delaware, began in 1769. Many wealthy Delawareans sent their children to schools elsewhere.

Soybeans (left) and fruit
are among Delaware's principal
agricultural products.

Unlike other states, Delaware did not make public education a top priority. The legislature established a fund for public schools in 1792. But it took Delaware until 1829—more than forty years after statehood—to establish a system of public schools. Today, a seven-member board of education, appointed by the governor, directs the state's public schools. The board's president has no definite term, but other members serve six-year terms. The board of education appoints the state superintendent of schools.

Delaware has about 63,000 elementary school students and 30,000 secondary school students. Private and parochial school enrollment account for about 23,000 students. There are about 6,000 public school teachers. Teachers receive an average salary of $27,500, and schools spend about $3,000 per student, both figures slightly above the national average.

The University of Delaware, located in the northwestern city of Newark, is the state's largest college. Delaware State College, originally a school for blacks, is located in Dover. Another state institution, Delaware Technical and Community College, has two-year campuses in Dover, Georgetown, Wilmington, and Newark. Private schools that offer four-year programs include Wilmington College, in New Castle; Goldey Beacom College, in Wilmington; and Wesley College, in Dover. The state also has scholarship programs for Delaware students who attend out-of-state colleges for programs not offered by schools within the state.

ECONOMY AND INDUSTRY

Principal Products:

Agriculture: Poultry, beef cattle, hogs, dairy products, corn, wheat, soybeans, potatoes, fruit, vegetables, nursery products

Manufacturing: Chemicals, oil refining, transportation equipment, building equipment, textiles

Natural Resources: Forest products, sand, gravel, kaolin, granite, gemstones, oysters

115

Summit Bridge crosses the Chesapeake and Delaware Canal west of St. Georges.

Business and Trade: Years ago, agriculture predominated in the small, rural
state of Delaware. Today, manufacturing is the most important part of the
economy. The du Pont family started a gunpowder company near Wilmington in
the early 1800s. Later, the du Ponts expanded into the manufacture of chemicals,
synthetic fibers, and other products. The chemical industry is so important in
Wilmington that the city is sometimes called the "Chemical Capital of the World."
Other important manufacturing industries in Delaware include food processing,
automobiles, nonelectrical machinery, rubber and plastic items, printed materials,
metal products, and textiles.

Tobacco once was Delaware's main agricultural product. But tobacco production
stripped the soil of nutrients, and eventually the colonists abandoned it. Poultry
now ranks as the state's top source of farm income. Sussex County, in southern
Delaware, is one of America's centers for broiler chickens, and Delaware ranks
among the top ten states in broiler production. Dairy farming provides another
valuable source of income. Delaware farmers also raise beef cattle and hogs. Truck
farming, providing fruits and vegetables to nearby urban areas, serves as another
important farm activity. Many Delaware farmers grow corn, wheat, and soybeans.
Some farmers make the holly wreaths that are popular at Christmastime.

Lumber and fishing provide two sources of income from the land. But although
mining of iron was important in colonial days, it is insignificant now. Delaware

ranks last among the states in value of mineral production. Sand, gravel, and clay are the main mineral products. The state also supplies gemstones and Brandywine blue granite, which sometimes is used as a decorative building stone.

Delaware, the "Corporate State," enjoys a unique source of income. The state's incorporation laws are less rigid than those of other states. Thus many companies choose to become Delaware corporations, although they may do little business there.

Wilmington, the major city, is the trading capital. Ships from around the continent and around the world dock here. At the other end of the state, the town of Seaford receives Nanticoke River traffic.

Transportation: Ever since colonial days, Delawareans have relied on water transportation. Even now, waterways provide important transit. The Delaware River gives Wilmington access to the Atlantic Ocean. The Chesapeake and Delaware Canal connects the river cities of Wilmington and Philadelphia to the Chesapeake Bay city of Baltimore. This canal separates the urban northern part of Delaware from the rural southern part. The Lewes and Rehoboth Canal connects the town of Lewes with Rehoboth Bay. A ferry from Lewes to Cape May, New Jersey, provides a linkup along highway U.S. 9 between the two states.

Delaware's first railroad, the New Castle and Frenchtown, was built in 1831. Over the next half century, many smaller lines appeared. But the emergence of highway travel spelled doom for most of these small railroads. Delaware now has only about 300 mi. (483 km) of railroad track. Wilmington, a stop on an Amtrak line between Philadelphia and Baltimore, is the only city with passenger service.

Most of the roads that crisscross Delaware are state roads. A small portion of I-95 in the northern part of the state is the only interstate highway. More important are federal roads. U.S. 301 links Newark and Blackbird. U.S. 113 connects Dover to Selbyville and the Maryland state line. U.S. 9 cuts from Laurel to Lewes. U.S. 13, Delaware's "main street," leads from the Wilmington area through the heart of the state to the southern border town of Delmar.

Delaware has about fifteen public and private airports. Greater Wilmington Airport, in New Castle, is the busiest commercial terminal. Dover Air Force Base near Dover serves as a major center for international armed forces flights.

Communication: Delaware's first successful newspaper, the *Delaware Gazette*, hit the presses in 1785. Today, the state has two daily newspapers—the *Morning News*, of Wilmington, and the *Delaware State News*, of Dover. About fifteen weeklies are also published in Delaware.

WDEL, of Wilmington, which went on the air in 1922, was the first Delaware radio station. Today, Delaware has about twenty commercial radio stations. WHYY-TV in Wilmington is the state's public television station. Delaware remains the only state without a commercial television station.

SOCIAL AND CULTURAL LIFE

Museums: Delaware retains a great pride in its heritage. That heritage shows in the state's museums. Perhaps the most notable is the Delaware State Museum, in Dover. It includes a gallery with changing exhibits on Delaware life, a floor with military, maritime and space exhibits, an 1880 gallery with shops of a hundred years ago, and a large collection of early phonographs and records. The Delaware Agricultural Museum, in Dover, traces farm life from the days of the early settlers. Island Field Historical Museum, near Dover, preserves a prehistoric burial site used by two early cultures. Hagley Museum, near Wilmington, on the historic site of the original E. I. du Pont black powder mills, depicts nineteenth-century community life. Old Town Hall, in Wilmington, shows exhibits pertaining to Delaware history, plus decorative arts, a restored jail, and a children's room. Science lovers can enjoy the Delaware Museum of Natural History, in Wilmington, with its impressive shell collection, Hall of Mammals, and Hall of Birds. The University of Delaware, at Newark, has a large collection of fossils and unusual minerals. Art enthusiasts enjoy Wilmington's Delaware Art Museum, with works by Delaware artists Howard Pyle and John Sloan, plus a large Andrew Wyeth collection. Winterthur Museum and Gardens, in Wilmington, features decorative arts from 1640 to 1860, a 200-acre (81-hectare) landscape reminiscent of an eighteenth-century English woodland, plus an untouched forest known as Charles Woods.

Libraries: Delaware's first library began in Wilmington in 1754. The city also led the way in libraries after statehood. In 1788, the Library Company of Wilmington created the Wilmington Institute Free Library, the oldest continuous library in the state. The University of Delaware's Morris Library, with some 1.5 million books, is the largest in the state. Other important libraries include the Hall of Records, in Dover, which contains the original charter for the Delaware territory; the Historical Society of Delaware, in Wilmington, with its many Delaware documents; and the Eleutherian Mills-Hagley Foundation, on the Brandywine. The Winterthur Museum contains a fine collection of books on America and the decorative arts. Du Pont and Hercules experimental stations at Wilmington, Newark, and Newport have large chemical libraries. The state has about thirty public libraries plus bookmobiles that reach the rural areas.

Performing Arts: Wilmington, the largest city, is also Delaware's cultural capital. It boasts a symphony orchestra and a drama league. The Grand Opera House, which serves as Delaware's Center for the Performing Arts, hosts theater, dance, music, opera, and film. The Playhouse, in Wilmington, presents theatrical road companies. Breck's Mill, on the Brandywine, offers performances by actors and musicians. The Village of Arden hosts productions by Shakespeare and Gilbert and Sullivan. Delaware's colleges also offer many performances.

Sports and Recreation: Delaware has not hosted a major-league sports team for more than a hundred years. In 1884, a Wilmington team played briefly in the ill-fated Union Association. But Delaware sports fans need not moan about the lack of nearby professional sports. Baseball fans are only a few miles from the Baltimore Orioles or the Philadelphia Phillies. Football fans cheer for the Philadelphia Eagles or the Washington Redskins. Basketball buffs follow the Philadelphia 76ers or the Washington Bullets. Hockey fans root for the Philadelphia Flyers or the Washington Capitals. Indoor soccer aficionados watch the Baltimore Blast. Racing is the big sport in the state. Brandywine and Harrington racetracks offer harness racing. Delaware Park, in Wilmington, provides thoroughbred racing. Dover

The Delaware Art Museum, in Wilmington

Downs has one track for auto racing and one for horse racing. College football fans can watch topflight teams at the University of Delaware and Delaware State College. Delawareans also take advantage of the outdoors. They camp, swim, or fish at any of the ten state parks or four state forests. Others enjoy fishing or boating along the coast, or sightseeing at Rehoboth Bay. Bombay Hook National Wildlife Refuge near Smyrna is a resting and feeding spot for migratory waterfowl in the fall and spring.

Historic Sites and Landmarks:

Barratt's Chapel, near Frederica, is the birthplace of the Methodist Episcopal church in America.

Belmont Hall, in Smyrna, was the home of colonial governor Thomas Collins.

Cooch's Bridge, near Newark, is the site of Delaware's only Revolutionary War battle and, according to tradition, the site where Betsy Ross's flag was first raised in battle.

John Dickinson Plantation, near Dover, is the restored colonial home of the "Penman of the Revolution."

119

The Old Swedes Church, in Wilmington, was founded in 1698.

Fort Christina Monument, near Wilmington, marks the first Swedish settlement in Delaware and contains a replica of a log cabin, a type of dwelling introduced by the Swedes to North America.

Fort Delaware State Park, near Delaware City, is a preserved fort built in 1859 that housed up to 12,500 Confederate prisoners during the Civil War.

Historic Houses of Odessa, Delaware, in Odessa, are four historic properties owned and operated by Winterthur Museum and Gardens; they include the 1774 Georgian *Corbit-Sharp House,* the 1769 *Wilson-Warner House,* the early-eighteenth-century *Collins-Sharp House,* and the *Brick Hotel Gallery.*

Holy Trinity (Old Swedes) Church, in Wilmington, was founded in 1698 and still conducts regular services.

Immanuel Episcopal Church, in New Castle, was founded in 1689; it is the site of the graves of many Delaware pioneers.

Kalmar Nyckel Museum and Shipyard, at Fort Christina Park near Wilmington, includes a working seventeenth-century shipyard; a museum; and a replica of the *Kalmar Nyckel,* the ship that brought the first permanent Swedish settlers to the Delaware Valley.

Lewes Restored Buildings include a lighthouse, a country store, a Coast Guard boathouse with marine exhibits, and a doctor's office.

Old Dutch House, in New Castle, is considered the oldest dwelling in the state.

Prince George's Chapel, in Bethany Beach, is a restored eighteenth-century church.

Other Interesting Places to Visit:

Bombay Hook National Wildlife Refuge, near Smyrna, is a major fall and spring resting place for migratory birds.

Brandywine Springs Park, near Wilmington, was the site of a once-famous resort hotel.

Cape May-Lewes Ferry, in Lewes, provides a water connection along highway U.S. 9 between Delaware and New Jersey.

The Circle, in Georgetown, is a circle-shaped park where each year winners and losers of elections dress in colonial costumes and greet each other on Return Day.

Dover Heritage Trail, in Dover, provides a walking tour of historic sites and other attractions in the Old Dover Historic District and the Victorian Dover Historic District.

Fenwick Lighthouse, on Fenwick Island, is a historic lighthouse built in 1857.

General Motors Corporation, in Wilmington, offers industrial tours.

The Green, in New Castle, is an old public square surrounded by historic buildings.

New Castle Court House, in New Castle, contains the dome that is exactly 12 miles (19 kilometers) from Delaware's curved northern border.

Octagonal Schoolhouse, near Dover, was one of Delaware's first free public schools.

Old State House, in Dover, is the second-oldest seat of government in continuous use.

Rehoboth Beach, with its fine sand and boardwalk attractions that lure visitors from Baltimore and Washington, D.C., is known as the "Nation's Summer Capital."

Rodney Square, in Wilmington, contains a statue that honors the famous ride to Philadelphia by Delaware's revolutionary hero, Caesar Rodney.

Wilmington and Western Railroad provides round-trip steam-train rides from the Greenbank Station through the scenic Red Clay Valley.

Zwaanendael Museum, in Lewes, exhibits colonial, Indian, and Dutch items in the uniquely designed building patterned after a town hall in the Netherlands.

IMPORTANT DATES

1609 — Henry Hudson, sailing for the Dutch East India Company, discovers Delaware Bay and the Delaware River

1610 — Captain Samuel Argall gives present Delaware Bay the name De La Warr Bay, after Lord De La Warr, governor of Virginia

1631 — The first colonists from Holland settle at Zwaanendael (site of present-day Lewes)

1632 — An argument with a Lenape chief brings about the death of Zwaanendael settlers

1638 — A Swedish expedition led by Peter Minuit arrives at The Rocks (present-day Wilmington) and establishes the first permanent settlement; the Dutch protest the right of Swedes to settle or trade on the Delaware River

1640 — Reorus Torkillus, the first Lutheran preacher in America, arrives at Fort Christina

1651 — Peter Stuyvesant, the Dutch governor of New Netherland, builds Fort Casimir at Sandhook (now New Castle)

1654 — Johan Classon Rising, governor of New Sweden, captures Fort Casimir and renames it Fort Trinity

1655 — Stuyvesant captures Fort Trinity and renames it Fort Casimir; Swedes surrender Fort Christina and all Swedish claims to the Dutch

1663 — Peter Cornelius Plockhoy establishes a Mennonite colony at Zwaanandael, near present-day Lewes

1664 — Sir Robert Carr seizes Delaware territory for the Duke of York

1673 — The Dutch regain control and establish courts at New Castle and Hoornkill, or Hoerekill (now Lewes)

1674 — Dutch North American possessions, including those in Delaware, pass to the British

1682 — The first court under William Penn, the new Quaker proprietary, meets

1698 — Pirates pillage Lewes

1699 — The crew of *Sweepstakes* mutinies at New Castle

1700 — Captain Kidd visits and trades at Lewes

The Zwaanendael Museum in Lewes, patterned after a town hall in The Netherlands, commemorates the first Dutch settlement in 1631.

1701 — The first survey of the curved boundary between Delaware and Pennsylvania is made with New Castle Court House as the center of the circle

1704 — The three Lower Counties under the charter of 1701 meet in their first assembly at New Castle

1711 — Gustavus Hesselius, first important painter in America, arrives at Old Swedes Church in Wilmington

1722 — Fire razes the home of Colonel John French, destroying the colony's legislature records

1735 — William Shipley, "Father of Wilmington," buys land in Wilmington

1738 — Wilmington becomes the Borough of Wilmington

1748 — The Old Friends Meeting House, in Wilmington, becomes a school, now the oldest continuously operating school in the state

1750 — The boundary commissioners decide on the spire of New Castle Court House as the center of a 12-mile (19-kilometer) boundary arc

1754 — The first library company is founded in Wilmington

1755 — The Friendship Fire Company, the state's first fire company, is organized in Wilmington

1767 — John Dickinson, the "Penman of the American Revolution," writes the first of his *Letters from a Farmer in Pennsylvania to the Inhabitants of the British Colonies*

123

1774—Thomas McKean, George Read, and Caesar Rodney are appointed delegates to the First Continental Congress

1776—Caesar Rodney, despite illness, rides from Dover to Philadelphia to break the tie between McKean and Read, and vote for independence; the first legislature under the new constitution meets in New Castle

1777—Dover becomes Delaware's capital; colonial troops fight the British at the Battle of Cooch's Bridge; at Wilmington, the British capture a boat containing Delaware documents and monies as well as Delaware president John McKinly

1781—Thomas McKean is elected president of the Continental Congress

1783—Richard Allen becomes the first black to preach in Wilmington

1784—The first Methodist services in America are conducted at Barratt's Chapel

1787—Delaware becomes the first state to ratify the Constitution, thus making it the first state in the Union; the legislature grants exclusive rights to John Fitch for a steamboat he invented and to Oliver Evans for a steam carriage he invented

1791—Wilmington schoolmaster Robert Coram publishes *Plan for the General Establishment of Schools Throughout the United States*

1792—Delaware adopts its second constitution, which replaces the 1776 document

1793—A yellow-fever plague sweeps Philadelphia, and the port of Wilmington profits from shippers wishing to avoid the disease

1795—Jacob Broom opens the state's first cotton factory in Old Academy

1798—The yellow-fever epidemic sweeps from Philadelphia into Wilmington

1802—Éleuthère Irénée du Pont de Nemours begins to manufacture gunpowder on land by Brandywine Creek

1807—Caesar A. Rodney serves as U.S. attorney general under President Thomas Jefferson

1813—The British shell Lewes during the War of 1812; the United Church of Africans, the first black-run church in the United States, is formed

1814—James A. Bayard signs the Treaty of Ghent, ending the War of 1812

1822—Brandywine Creek rises, breaking a dam and destroying mills

1824—Blacks form the African School Society of Wilmington to educate their children

1829 — The Chesapeake and Delaware Canal opens

1831 — Delaware adopts its third constitution

1833 — Louis McLane is appointed U.S. secretary of state

1849 — John M. Clayton is appointed U.S. secretary of state

1871 — An earthquake shakes Wilmington and the surrounding area

1885 — Thomas F. Bayard is appointed U.S. secretary of state

1893 — Delaware receives "The Wedge," a small piece of northern land, in a boundary dispute with Maryland; Thomas F. Bayard is appointed the first ambassador to Great Britain

1895 — The General Assembly adjourns without electing a U.S. senator, an attempt to block John Edward Addicks

1897 — Delaware adopts its fourth constitution

1900 — Illustrator Howard Pyle opens a school of art at Wilmington

1905 — Delaware becomes the last state to abolish the use of a pillory as punishment

1938 — J. P. Marquand wins the Pulitzer Prize in fiction for *The Late George Apley*

1963 — The Delaware Turnpike John F. Kennedy Memorial Highway opens, completing a nonstop highway between Boston and Washington, D.C.

1971 — The Delaware Coastal Zone Act prohibits construction of industrial plants on coastal areas

1978 — Daniel Nathans wins the Nobel Prize in physiology or medicine for his work with molecular hormones

1984 — S. B. Woo is elected lieutenant governor, becoming the highest-ranking Asian-American official in the United States

1988 — Two Delaware politicians, Pierre "Pete" du Pont and Joseph Biden, make short-lived bids for the U.S. presidency

RICHARD ALLEN

JAMES BAYARD

GUNNING BEDFORD, JR.

IMPORTANT PEOPLE

James Adams (1725?-1792), printer; Delaware resident from 1761; set up the state's first printing press, in Wilmington; published important early books and documents, including John Filson's book, *The Discovery, Settlement, and Present State of Kentucke*

John Edward O'Sullivan Addicks (1841-1919), politician; Delaware resident from 1888; gained wealth from financing and building gas works in many cities; tried—unsuccessfully—for nearly twenty years to be elected a U.S. senator from Delaware

Richard Allen (1760-1831), born a slave near Dover; religious leader; founded the African Methodist Episcopal church, the first black church in the United States; founded the Free African Society, an important social welfare group

Richard Bassett (1745-1815), lawyer, statesman; Kent County landholder, resident of Dover; signed the U.S. Constitution and helped make Delaware the first colony to ratify the document; U.S. senator (1789-93); chief justice, Delaware court of common pleas (1793-99); governor (1799-1801)

James Asheton Bayard (1767-1815), statesman; helped negotiate the Treaty of Ghent, which ended the War of 1812; played a pivotal role in deciding the presidential election of 1800 for Thomas Jefferson; U.S. representative from Delaware (1797-1803); U.S. senator from Delaware (1805-13)

Thomas Francis Bayard (1828-1898), born in Wilmington; politician; U.S. senator (1869-85); U.S. secretary of state (1885-89); gained a reputation for high ideals and unquestioned honesty; U.S. ambassador to Britain (1893-97)

Gunning Bedford, Jr. (1747-1812), lawyer, statesman; resident of Dover from 1779; spoke out for rights of small states at the Constitutional Convention of 1787; led the Great Compromise, which gave each state equal votes in the Senate

John Bernard (1756-1828), actor, producer; headed the first theater troop in Delaware

Valerie Bertinelli (1960-   ), born in Wilmington; actress; starred in the television comedies "One Day at a Time" and "Sydney"

Joseph Robinette Biden, Jr. (1942-   ), politician; U.S. senator from Delaware (1973-   ); conducted Senate Judiciary Committee hearings on the Supreme Court nomination of Robert Bork

Robert Montgomery Bird (1806-1854), born in New Castle; physician, playwright, novelist; wrote plays, including *The Gladiator*; wrote *Nick of the Woods* and *Hawks of Hawk Hollow*, which attempted to treat the frontier realistically

Blackbeard (?-1718), born Edward Teach; pirate; terrorized the Atlantic Coast in the early 1700s; stored his booty in a hideaway at Blackbird Creek; died in a fight with men from the Virginia ship *Pearl*

Jacob Broom (1752-1810), born in Wilmington; surveyor, statesman; built the first cotton mill on Brandywine Creek; delegate to the Constitutional Convention of 1787

Henry Seidel Canby (1878-1961), born in Wilmington; journalist, author; founded the *Saturday Review* magazine; wrote *Classic Americans*, a review of important literary figures, and *Our House*, a novel

Annie Jump Cannon (1863-1941), born in Dover; astronomer; compiled a reference of over 200,000 stars; discovered 300 variable stars, 5 double stars, and 5 novas; gained the title "Census Taker of the Sky"

William Cannon (1809-1865), born in Bridgeville; merchant, statesman; persuaded Delaware to remain with the Union during the Civil War; governor (1863-65)

Wallace Hume Carothers (1896-1937), chemist; developed nylon while working for the Du Pont Company

Robert R. M. Carpenter (1915-   ), born in New Castle; baseball owner; purchased weak Philadelphia Phillies franchise during World War II and turned it into one of strongest teams in the major leagues; helped the Phillies win the pennant (1950) and their first world championship (1980)

John Middleton Clayton (1796-1856), born in Dagsboro, Sussex County; politician; U.S. senator (1829-36, 1845-49, 1853-56); chief justice of Delaware (1837-39); U.S. secretary of state (1849-50); negotiated Clayton-Bulwer Treaty, which settled border disputes with England; helped open trade relations with the Orient

Felix Octavius Carr Darley (1822-1888), illustrator; while living in Claymont, he illustrated special editions of the works of Charles Dickens, James Fenimore Cooper, and William Shakespeare

VALERIE BERTINELLI

ANNIE JUMP CANNON

WALLACE CAROTHERS

FELIX O. C. DARLEY

DAVID PIETERSEN DE VRIES

JOHN DICKINSON

PIERRE S. DU PONT

DALLAS GREEN

David Pietersen De Vries (1592?-1655?), seaman; organized the first European colony in the Delaware valley, at Zwaanendael (now Lewes)

John Dickinson (1732-1808), author, statesman; became known as the "Penman of the Revolution"; wrote *Letters from a Farmer in Pennsylvania,* which protested the Townshend Acts; president of Delaware (1781); delegate from Delaware to the Constitutional Convention of 1787; under the pseudonym "Fabius," he wrote letters persuading Delaware and Pennsylvania to ratify the Constitution

Éleuthère Irénée du Pont (1771-1834), industrialist; founded the gunpowder works that led to the present-day Du Pont Company; built his first plant on the Brandywine River, near Wilmington; introduced Spanish merino sheep to improve American wool

Henry Algernon du Pont (1838-1926), born near Wilmington; military officer, politician; U.S. senator (1906-17); led the Senate Military Committee (1911-13)

Henry Francis du Pont (1880-1969), born in Wilmington; horticulturist; collector of Americana; founder of the Winterthur Museum and Gardens

Pierre Samuel du Pont (1870-1954), born in Wilmington; industrialist; president (1915-19) and board chairman (1919-40) of Du Pont; president of General Motors (1920-23); made substantial donations to schools and hospitals

Pierre Samuel "Pete" du Pont IV (1935-   ), born in Wilmington; lawyer, politician; U.S. representative (1971-77); governor (1977-85); helped revise banking laws to encourage out-of-state banks to move to Delaware

Thomas Coleman du Pont (1863-1930), industrialist, philanthropist, politician; as president of Du Pont (1902-15), he formalized research and began incentive bonuses, pension plans, and safety bonuses; U.S. senator from Delaware (1921-22, 1925-28); gained the title "Father of the Superhighway" by using his own funds to build a forerunner of the modern turnpike the length of Delaware (1924)

Oliver Evans (1755-1819), born in Newport; inventor; built what probably was America's first self-propelled land vehicle; invented a high-pressure steam engine; his inventions revolutionized the milling process

Thomas Garrett (1789-1871), abolitionist; resident of Wilmington; helped about three thousand slaves escape by using his home as a station on the Underground Railroad

George Gray (1840-1925), born in New Castle; politician, jurist; U.S. senator (1885-99); judge of the U.S. Circuit Court of Appeals

George Dallas Green (1934-   ), born in Newport; professional baseball player and manager; managed the Philadelphia Phillies to the team's first world championship (1980); as general manager of the Chicago Cubs made trades that helped the team win the National League East Division title (1984)

Willard Hall (1780-1875), jurist and educator; resident of Wilmington from 1803; prepared a code of law for Delaware; helped organize Delaware's public school system

Henry Hudson (?-1611), explorer; discovered Delaware Bay while sailing for the Dutch East India Company; helped establish claims to New World lands

HENRY HUDSON

William Julius "Judy" Johnson (1899-1989), professional baseball player; grew up in Wilmington; starred at third base for the great Pittsburgh Crawfords and Homestead Grays teams of the Negro League; retired with an estimated .344 lifetime batting average; as a scout for Braves and Phillies, helped young black players enter the major leagues; entered Baseball Hall of Fame (1975)

John Lofland (1798-1849), born in Milford; author; wrote poems and stories with Delaware settings, especially the Brandywine Creek area; wrote *Harp of Delaware*, a poetry collection; known as the "Milford Bard"

WILLIAM "JUDY" JOHNSON

Thomas Macdonough (1783-1825), born in The Trap (now Macdonough); naval officer; captured the entire British fleet in the 1814 Battle of Plattsburgh; stopped an enemy invasion from Canada; gained the nickname "Hero of Lake Champlain"

John Phillips Marquand (1893-1960), born in Wilmington; novelist; wrote stories showing that inheritors of wealth do not understand social change; won the 1938 Pulitzer Prize in fiction for *The Late George Apley*; wrote *H. M. Pulham, Esquire*; *Point of No Return*; and Mr. Moto stories

THOMAS MACDONOUGH

Thomas McKean (1734-1817), statesman; signed the Declaration of Independence as a delegate from Delaware; member (1774-83) and president (1781) of the Continental Congress; wrote most of the original Delaware constitution; president of Delaware (1777); wrote (with James Wilson) *Commentaries on the Constitution of the United States of America*

John Joseph "Sadie" McMahon (1867-1954), born in Rising Sun; professional baseball player; pitched for Baltimore teams in the American Association and the National League; won 20 or more games per season from 1890 to 1894, including 36 in 1890; led the Baltimore Orioles to three pennants in the 1890s

JOHN P. MARQUAND

Stephen Wallis "Pop" Merihew (1862-1947), born in Wilmington; journalist; published *ALT*, a journal that helped popularize lawn tennis in the United States; wrote *The Quest for the Davis Cup*

JOHN B. MOORE

DANIEL NATHANS

GEORGE READ

JUDGE REINHOLD

Peter Minuit (1580-1638), explorer; as a Dutch colonial governor, he bought Manhattan Island from Algonquian Indians for trinkets worth $24; led a 1638 Swedish expedition to North America and built Fort Christina (now Wilmington)

John Bassett Moore (1860-1947), born in Smyrna; jurist; the first American judge of the Permanent Court of International Justice (1921-28)

Daniel Nathans (1928-   ), born in Wilmington; scientist; shared the 1978 Nobel Prize in medicine for his research on molecular genetics

Hezekiah Niles (1777-1839), journalist; owned a printing shop in Wilmington; moved to Baltimore and published *Niles' Weekly Register*, a political magazine

William Penn (1644-1718), colonial leader; received rights for land west of the Delaware River from New York to Maryland; permitted religious freedom in his colony of Pennsylvania; established a separate government for the Three Lower Counties of Delaware

Howard Pyle (1853-1911), born in Wilmington; writer, illustrator; wrote and illustrated *The Merrie Adventures of Robin Hood, Howard Pyle's Book of Pirates*, and *The Price of Blood*

George Read (1733-1798), statesman; signed both the Declaration of Independence and the U.S. Constitution as a representative of Delaware; served in nearly every important office in Delaware during colonial and early statehood years; influenced government throughout Delaware and the new nation; U.S. senator (1789-93); chief justice of Delaware (1793-98)

Jay Saunders Redding (1906-   ), born in Wilmington; educator, author; wrote and reviewed material dealing with black historical and cultural themes; wrote *On Being Negro in America, To Make a Poet Black*, and *They Came in Chains*

Judge Reinhold (1956-   ), born in Wilmington; actor; appeared in *Beverly Hills Cop, Ruthless People*, and *Fast Times at Ridgemont High*

Caesar Rodney (1728-1784), born in Dover; statesman; member of Continental Congress (1774-76, 1777, 1778); rode all night from Dover to Philadelphia to cast Delaware's deciding vote for independence in 1776; major general of Delaware militia during the Revolutionary War; president of Delaware (1778-82)

William V. Roth, Jr. (1921-   ), politician; U.S. representative from Delaware (1967-71); U.S. senator (1971-   ); proposed the Kemp-Roth bill, which would lower income taxes by 10 percent each year for three years

Christopher Short (1937-   ), born in Milford; professional baseball player; pitcher who won 135 major-league games for the Philadelphia Phillies and the Milwaukee Brewers; won 20 games in 1966; played in two All-Star games

Upton Sinclair (1878-1968), writer and social reformer; lived in the "single tax" village of Arden; wrote *The Jungle*, which exposed conditions in the meat-packing industry and led to pure food laws; won the 1943 Pulitzer Prize in fiction for *Dragon's Teeth*; helped organize the American Civil Liberties Union and the League for Industrial Democracy

UPTON SINCLAIR

Peter Stuyvesant (1610?-1672), Dutch explorer and colonizer; led the forces that took control of New Sweden, which included Delaware and parts of New Jersey and Pennsylvania; made the New Sweden colonies part of New Netherland; lost the New Netherland colony to the English

Henry Lea Tatnall (1829-1885), born in Brandywine Village; painter; created landscapes that celebrate the countryside and waters of the Brandywine area

Sydenham Thorne (1747-1793), minister; helped found Milford and tended to its nearby Christ Church

PETER STUYVESANT

George Thorogood (1951-   ), musician; started performing with bands in the Wilmington area; led the Delaware Destroyers in hard-driving rock-and-roll songs; recorded "Bad to the Bone" and "Nobody but Me"

George Alfred Townsend (1841-1914), born in Georgetown; author; penned vivid reports of the Civil War; wrote many articles under the pen name "Gath"; wrote *Tales of the Chesapeake*, a series of folktales, and *The Entailed Hat*, a novel about the notorious Patty Cannon

GEORGE THOROGOOD

Francis Vincent (1822-1884), author, reformer; published the weekly newspaper *Blue Hen's Chicken* and served as leader of many progressive causes; established life-saving stations on the Delaware coast; favored abolition of slavery, toll-free bridges, and shorter hours for women workers; in 1870, he proposed a league for peace in Europe

Christopher Ward (1868-1944), born in Wilmington; author; wrote parodies such as *The Triumph of the Nut*, and history-based novels such as *The Dutch and Swedes on the Delaware* and *The Saga of Captain John Smith*

John Williams (1904-1988), born in Frankford; politician; was a U.S. senator longer than any other Delawarean (1947-71); became known for his honesty, independent views, and opposition to graft and corruption

JOHN WILLIAMS

S. B. WOO

Victor Willis (1876-1947), professional baseball player; lived in Wilmington; pitcher who won 247 major-league games with the Boston Braves, the Pittsburgh Pirates, and the St. Louis Cardinals; led the Pirates to the 1909 National League pennant

James Harrison Wilson (1837-1925), soldier; lived near Wilmington; commanded one of the largest Union forces during the Civil War; captured Confederate President Jefferson Davis

S. B. Woo (1942-   ), scientist, politician; as lieutenant-governor of Delaware (1985-89), was the highest-ranking Asian-American politician in the nation

GOVERNORS

Thomas Collins	1786-1789	James Ponder	1871-1875
Jehu Davis	1789	John P. Cochran	1875-1879
Joshua Clayton	1789-1796	John W. Hall	1879-1883
Gunning Bedford	1796-1797	Charles C. Stockley	1883-1887
Daniel Rogers	1797-1799	Benjamin T. Biggs	1887-1891
Richard Bassett	1799-1801	Robert J. Reynolds	1891-1895
James Sykes	1801-1802	Joshua H. Marvil	1895
David Hall	1802-1805	William T. Watson	1895-1897
Nathaniel Mitchell	1805-1808	Ebe W. Tunnell	1897-1901
George Truitt	1808-1811	John Hunn	1901-1905
Joseph Haslet	1811-1814	Preston Lea	1905-1909
Daniel Rodney	1814-1817	Simeon S. Pennewell	1909-1913
John Clark	1817-1820	Charles R. Miller	1913-1917
Jacob Stout	1820-1821	John G. Townsend, Jr.	1917-1921
John Collins	1821-1822	William D. Denney	1921-1925
Caleb Rodney	1822-1823	Robert P. Robinson	1925-1929
Joseph Haslet	1823	C. Douglass Buck	1929-1937
Charles Thomas	1823-1824	Richard C. McMullen	1937-1941
Samuel Paynter	1824-1827	Walter W. Bacon	1941-1949
Charles Polk	1827-1830	Elbert N. Carvel	1949-1953
David Hazzard	1830-1833	James Caleb Boggs	1953-1960
Caleb P. Bennett	1833-1836	David P. Buckson	1960-1961
Charles Polk	1836-1837	Elbert N. Carvel	1961-1965
Cornelius P. Comegys	1837-1841	Charles L. Terry, Jr.	1965-1969
William B. Cooper	1841-1845	Russell W. Peterson	1969-1973
Thomas Stockton	1845-1846	Sherman W. Tribbitt	1973-1977
Joseph Maull	1846	Pierre S. du Pont	1977-1985
William Temple	1846-1847	Michael N. Castle	1985-
William Tharp	1847-1851		
William H. Ross	1851-1855		
Peter Causey	1855-1859		
William Burton	1859-1863		
William Cannon	1863-1865		
Gove Saulsbury	1865-1871		

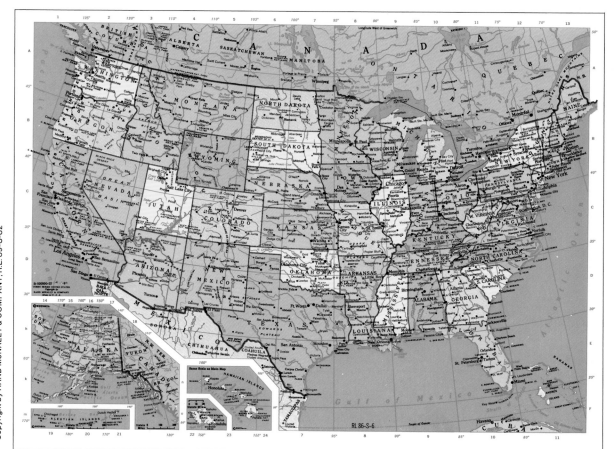

© Copyright by RAND McNALLY & COMPANY, R.L. 89-S-82

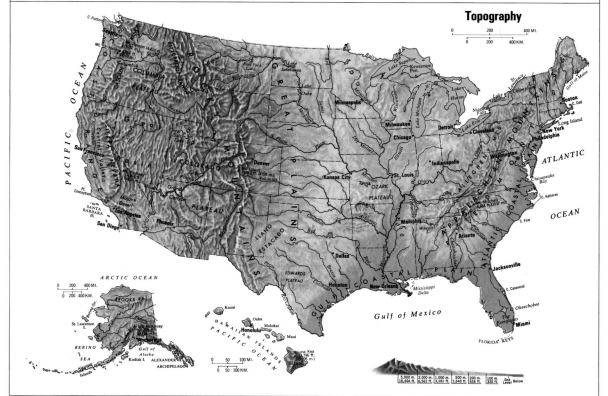

Topography

Courtesy of Hammond, Incorporated Maplewood, New Jersey

MAP KEY

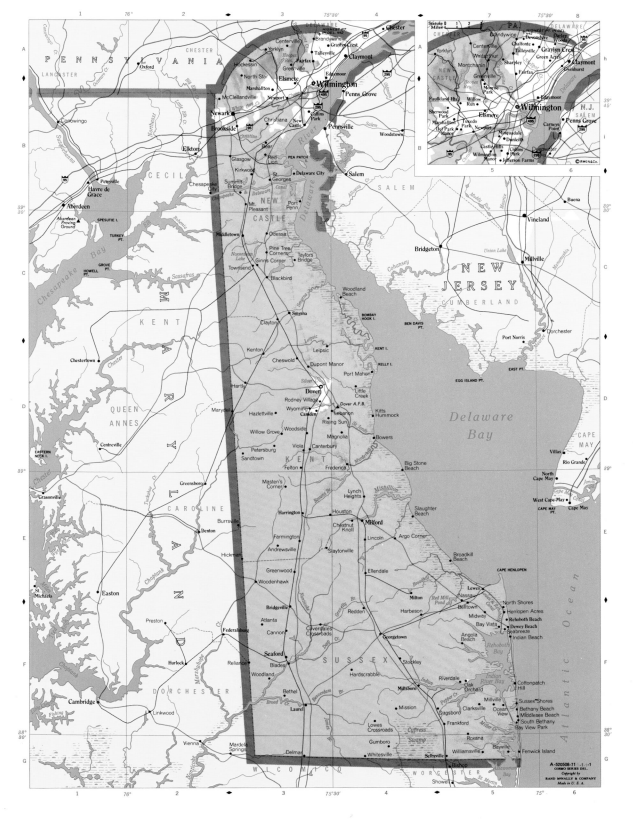

From Cosmopolitan World Atlas © 1990 by Rand McNally, R.L. 90-S-252

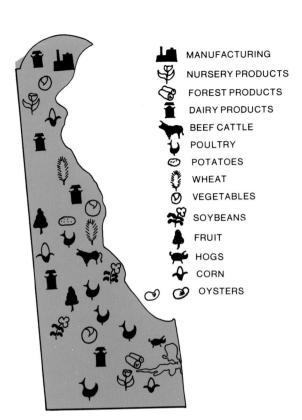

MANUFACTURING	
NURSERY PRODUCTS	
FOREST PRODUCTS	
DAIRY PRODUCTS	
BEEF CATTLE	
POULTRY	
POTATOES	
WHEAT	
VEGETABLES	
SOYBEANS	
FRUIT	
HOGS	
CORN	
OYSTERS	

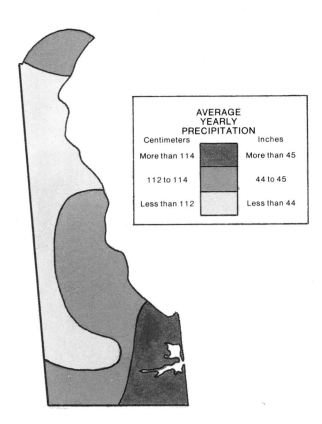

AVERAGE
YEARLY
PRECIPITATION

Centimeters		Inches
More than 114		More than 45
112 to 114		44 to 45
Less than 112		Less than 44

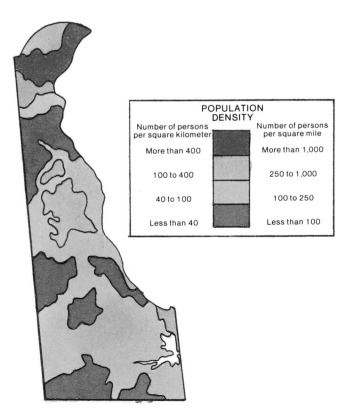

POPULATION
DENSITY

Number of persons per square kilometer	Number of persons per square mile
More than 400	More than 1,000
100 to 400	250 to 1,000
40 to 100	100 to 250
Less than 40	Less than 100

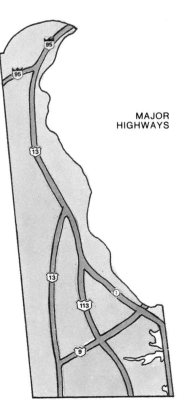

MAJOR
HIGHWAYS

TOPOGRAPHY

Courtesy of Hammond, Incorporated
Maplewood, New Jersey

5,000 m. | 2,000 m. | 1,000 m. | 500 m. | 200 m. | 100 m. | Sea
16,404 ft. | 6,562 ft. | 3,281 ft. | 1,640 ft. | 656 ft. | 328 ft. | Level | Below

442 ft. (135 m.)

Wilmington

Cumberland

Hagerstown

BLUE RIDGE

CATOCTIN MTN.

ALLEGHENY MTS.

APPALACHIAN MTS.

Potomac

N. Br.

Potomac

Backbone
Mtn.
3,360 ft.
(1,024 m.)

PIEDMONT PLATEAU

Aberdeen

Baltimore

Rockville

Potomac

Kent

Dover

Delaware
Bay

Annapolis

Washington

Delmarva

Choptank

Nanticoke

C. Henlopen

D.C.

Chesapeake Bay

Potomac

Peninsula

Cambridge

Salisbury

Assateague
Island

Pocomoke

COA

Tangier Sd.

Potomac

Pt.
Lookout

Chincoteague Bay

COUNTIES

Wilmington •

N E W   C A S T L E

DOVER ⊛

K E N T

S U S S E X

• Georgetown

Sunset, Little Assawoman Bay

INDEX

Page numbers that appear in boldface type indicate illustrations

138

The Old Dutch House, in New Castle, is considered to be the finest example of Dutch colonial architecture in Delaware.

Picture Identifications

Front cover: The Hagley Museum, on Brandywine Creek near Wilmington
Back cover: A street in historic New Castle
Pages 2-3: Surf fishing at Delaware Seashore State Park
Page 6: A 350th-anniversary reenactment of the Swedes landing at Delaware
Pages 8-9: Corn fields and hay fields near Centerville, the highest point in the state
Pages 18-19: Montage of Delawareans
Pages 24-25: A painting by Robert E. Goodier, A.W.S., W.H.S., of the Swedish settlers' arrival in 1638
Pages 44-45: *Delaware Water Gap*, an 1861 oil painting by George Inness
Pages 58-59: Architecture, downtown Wilmington
Pages 70-71: An oil refinery in Delaware City
Pages 82-83: Steeplechase racing at Point to Point, Winterthur Museum's annual outdoor event
Pages 90-91: Granogue, one of the du Pont family's mansions, on Brandywine Creek north of Wilmington
Page 108: Montage showing the state flag, state tree (American holly), state flower (peach blossom), and state insect (ladybug)

About the Author

Deborah Kent grew up in Little Falls, New Jersey, and received a Bachelor of Arts degree in English from Oberlin College in Ohio. She earned a Master's degree from Smith College School for Social Work, and spent four years working at the University Settlement in New York City.

Ms. Kent began work on her first book, a novel for young adults, in San Miguel de Allende, Mexico, where she lived for five years. She has written a dozen novels and contributed several books to the *America the Beautiful* series. She lives in Chicago with her husband and their daughter Janna.

Picture Acknowledgments

Front cover, © Forbert/**SuperStock**; 2-3, © **Carl Kleinschmidt Photography**; 4, © **Carl Kleinschmidt Photography**; 5, © Eric G. Carle/**SuperStock**; 6, © **Image Source, Inc.**; 8-9, © **Kevin Fleming**; 11, © **Mae Scanlan**; 12, © Eric Crossan/**Marilyn Gartman Agency**; 13, © **Carl Kleinschmidt Photography**; 14 (left), © Skip Moody/**M.L. Dembinsky, Jr. Photography Associates**; 14 (right), © **Kevin Fleming**; 15 (left), © Skip Moody/**M.L. Dembinsky, Jr. Photography Associates**; 15 (right), © Skip Moody/**M.L. Dembinsky, Jr. Photography Associates**; 16, © **Kevin Fleming**; 17, © **Kevin Fleming**; 18 (top left), © **Mary Ann Brockman**; 18 (top right), © Eric Crossan/**Marilyn Gartman Agency**; 18 (bottom left and bottom right), © **Carl Kleinschmidt Photography**; 19 (top left and bottom left), © **Carl Kleinschmidt Photography**; 19 (top right), © **Lisa J. Goodman**; 19 (bottom right), © **Jeff Greenberg**; 21, © **Kevin Fleming**; 22, © **Carl Kleinschmidt Photography**; 23 (left), © **Kevin Fleming**; 23 (right) © **Lisa J. Goodman**; 24-25, Courtesy of Bank of Delaware, Robert E. Goodier, A.W.S., W.H.S., artist; 27, **Historical Pictures Service, Chicago**; 29, **From the Permanent Collection of the University of Delaware**; 30, Courtesy of the Historical Society of Delaware; 31, Courtesy of the Historical Society of Delaware; 32, © Bill Howe/**Photri**; 33, © **J.L.G. Ferris, Archives of 76, Bay Village, Ohio**; 34, © **J.L.G. Ferris, Archives of 76, Bay Village, Ohio**; 35, **North Wind Picture Archives**; 36, **Historical Pictures Service, Chicago**; 37, © R. J. Bennett/**H. Armstrong Roberts**; 38, **Historical Pictures Service, Chicago**; 39 (left), Courtesy of the Historical Society of Delaware; 39 (right), **North Wind Picture Archives**; 40, © **Mary Ann Brockman**; 41, **Delaware State Archives**; 43, Courtesy of Bank of Delaware, Robert E. Goodier, A.W.S., W.H.S., artist; 44-45, **The Metropolitan Museum of Art, Morris K. Jesup Fund, 1932**; 47, © **Mae Scanlan**; 48, Courtesy of the Hagley Museum and Library; 49, Courtesy of the Historical Society of Delaware; 51, **Historical Pictures Service, Chicago**; 52, © Bob Glander/**SuperStock**; 53, © Bill Howe/**Photri**; 54, Courtesy of the Hagley Museum and Library; 55, Courtesy of the Hagley Museum and Library; 57, Courtesy of the Hagley Museum and Library; 58-59, © **Carl Kleinschmidt Photography**; 61, **AP/Wide World Photos**; 62, © **Mae Scanlan**; 65, © **Cameramann International, Ltd.**; 66, **AP/Wide World Photos**; 69 (both pictures), **UPI/Bettmann**; 70-71, © **Carl Kleinschmidt Photography**; 73, © David Forbert/**SuperStock**; 74, © Robert J. Bennett/**Photri**; 75, © **Mae Scanlan**; 76, Courtesy of the Historical Society of Delaware; 77, **Delaware Tourism Office**; 78, © **Judy Colbert**; 79 (left), © Robert J. Bennett/**Root Resources**; 79 (top right), © **Bob Willis**; 79 (bottom right), © Robert J. Bennett/**Photri**; 80 (left), © **Kevin Fleming**; 80 (right), © **Cameramann International, Ltd.**; 81 (both pictures), © **Kevin Fleming**; 82-83, © **Lisa J. Goodman**; 85, **Delaware Art Museum, Wilmington Purchase 1912**; 87 (left), Courtesy Private Collection; 87 (right), Collection of the Brandywine River Museum. Gift of Amanda K. Berls; 88, © **Kevin Fleming**; 90-91, © **Kevin Fleming**; 93 (left), © **Mary Ann Brockman**; 93 (map), **Len Meents**; 94, © A. Bolesta/**H. Armstrong Roberts**; 95, © Forbert/**SuperStock**; 96 (top and bottom left), © **Kevin Fleming**; 96 (bottom right), © W. Metzen/**H. Armstrong Roberts**; 98 (left), © Wendell Metzen/**H. Armstrong Roberts**; 98 (right), © R. Krubner/**H. Armstrong Roberts**; 99 (left), © J. Irwin/**H. Armstrong Roberts**; 99 (map), **Len Meents**; 100, © **SuperStock**; 101, **Delaware Tourism Office**; 102, © **Carl Kleinschmidt Photography**; 103 (left), © **Kevin Fleming**; 103 (map), **Len Meents**; 104, © Robert J. Bennett/**Photri**; 105, © R. J. Bennett/**H. Armstrong Roberts**; 107, © **Kevin Fleming**; 108 (background), © Kitty Kohout/**Root Resources**; 108 (flower), © **Kohout Productions**/**Root Resources**; 108 (ladybug), © **SuperStock**; 108 (flag), **Courtesy Flag Research Center, Winchester, Massachusetts, 01890**; 110, © **Photri**; 113, © **Kevin Fleming**; 115 (left), © Eric Crossan/**Marilyn Gartman Agency**; 115 (right), © Robert J. Bennett/**Photri**; 116, © Eric Crossan/**Marilyn Gartman Agency**; 119, © **Judy Colbert**; 120, © **SuperStock**; 123, © Robert J. Bennett/**Photri**; 126 (top), **The Library Company of Philadelphia**; 126 (middle), **Historical Pictures Service, Chicago**; 126 (bottom), **AP/Wide World Photos**; 127 (Bertinelli and Carothers), **AP/Wide World Photos**; 127 (Cannon), **Harvard College Observatory**; 127 (Darley), **North Wind Picture Archives**; 128 (De Vries and Dickinson), **North Wind Picture Archives**; 128 (du Pont and Green), **AP/Wide World Photos**; 129 (Hudson, Johnson, and Marquand), **AP/Wide World Photos**; 129 (Macdonough), **Historical Pictures Service, Chicago**; 130 (all four pictures), **AP/Wide World Photos**; 131 (Sinclair and Thorogood), **AP/Wide World Photos**; 131 (Stuyvesant), **Historical Pictures Service, Chicago**; 131 (Williams), **Senator John J. Williams Papers, University of Delaware Library**; 132, **Photograph by University of Delaware Photographic Services**; 138, © Lani Howe/**Photri**; 141, © Robert J. Bennett/**Root Resources**; Back cover, © **Mary Ann Brockman**

144